A View from the Hill

TRADING THE COURTROOM FOR AN IVORY TOWER

ROBERT V. WILLS

LEMON LANE PRESS • SANTA ANA, CALIFORNIA

Lemon Lane Press
1811 Beverly Glen Drive
Santa Ana, CA 92705
(714) 544-0344

www.maralys.com

Library of Congress Control Number 2012933345

Interior image of Bonally Tower by permission of Dover Publications, Inc.

Cover design: Stephanie Starr

Printed in the United States of America

Praise for *A View from the Hill*

Bob Wills' series of essays in *A View from the Hill*
make fascinating reading. His insightful and timely
essays cover a spectrum of topics from the political and
economic state of the planet to the social and ethical
systems of the day. Thought-provoking ... they're
worth your time.

William Kropp, Ph.D.,
Research physicist

Prepare to have your lapels grabbed by this pithy
volume! You'll find opinionated, witty, thought-
provoking perspectives generated by a razor-sharp
intellect focused on politics, the human condition, and
the future of our country and our world.

Jevelyn Yonchar, M.D.

Well-written and researched, sometimes reflective
and melancholic, often direct and audacious, always
intelligent and thought-provoking, his essays, for a
moment, stop me in my tracks. Make me think. Make
me wonder. Make me say out loud: Amen!

Bernardine Wilcox, M.P.T.

After years of hearing this brilliant lawyer's wisdom
and insights, I'm happy to see it down on paper for all
of us to share. A treat to read an original viewpoint.

Elaine Weinberg, J.D.

Robert Wills' essays are consistently thought-provoking, covering a wide and varied range of subjects. His writing style is succinct and compelling. Based on the author's life experiences, and coupled with his wide range of knowledge and quick recall of facts, the essays always ring true. I eagerly await each new one!

Linda R. Mayeda, M.A.

Only Bob Wills, a lawyer with his own law firm, could write the book, *Lawyers Are Killing America*, and make it convincing as well as fascinating. I couldn't put it down. Wills often sees how the nation or the world must change, and makes a case which convinces and captures the reader. Bob's new book will be a winner.

Allan Klumpp, M.A.
Engineer
Apollo Lunar Descent Guidance

A View from the Hill gives the reader a look into the mind of a great thinker. Bob's thoughts on young and old, red and blue, small pleasures and great calamities, are a gift to behold. With his mixture of sharp prose and just plain common sense, you will find yourself savoring these essays, and thinking of them long after you've finished this book.

Beth Strayer Handweiler, C.S.R.

Contents

Acknowledgements

S HOW ME A WORDSMITH and I'll show you someone who doesn't suffer editing lightly. The fact
that I allowed Maralys to tinker a bit with some of my
sentences in these pieces is no testimony to my good
nature. Rather, it's a tribute to her evolved skill as an
editor and manuscript polisher. And a payback for some
of the nuggets I've planted in her thirteen books....

Maralys also runs the computer in this house and
got my prose to the printer in apple pie order. So she
gets double points for editing and production.

Brad Hagen gets one Brownie point for buying
an Alpha Smart keyboard for Maralys, only because I
commandeered it and do all my writing on it.

Allene Symons will get a golden premium point
and three free copies of this little book if she turns out
another pretty little collector-quality volume.

FOREWORD

THE GOLDEN YEARS AREN'T ALWAYS GOLDEN, but retirement does offer a few bonuses.

Since I dissolved my law firm and sold our office building, I've had more time to reflect on the passing parade and record some critical impressions. Hopefully, having gathered eight decades of memories and having lived in diverse habitats and work environments has enhanced my perspective. It's probably not a coincidence that my degrees come in three diverse fields of study, and that my professional career ranged from corporate counsel, to medical malpractice trial attorney, to securities investor. And that our travels have ranged over four continents.

Any reader other than a friend or relative will soon find it difficult to believe that I am still registered as a Republican in Orange County, because I share so few views with 21st Century Republicans—and my disgust with them since Reagan is so explicit. Since politics is so pervasive in modern American life, I don't see how anyone examining his own life or his society can ignore it for long.

And I haven't.

So in today's polarized society, I have to warn any red-white-and-blue, God-fearing, card-carrying member of the Grand Old Party to proceed further with caution lest he or she take my views as a personal assault. Or suffer the same epiphany that I did when, in the early 1980s, the Gipper became the hallowed leader of the Free World.

Aside from American politics, I hope that my forays into ethics, sociology, and philosophy do cover a wider range of vantage points than average and that my crystal ball isn't too cloudy. I threw away my rose-colored glasses about 40 years ago, and wonder if any cockeyed optimist today is in touch with reality.

Meanwhile, thanks for dropping by.

Robert V. Wills

Chapter 1

Weasel Words Unlimited:
The U.S. Constitution

I AM ALWAYS BEMUSED, and often irritated, when rock-ribbed, red-white-and-blue stalwarts declare that what we need are judges and politicians who "follow the Constitution," page, chapter, and verse. They are usually grousing about some new social or economic decision that doesn't suit their political posture.

Have they ever read the U.S. Constitution, word for word? The document is simple, well-intentioned, two centuries old, and jam-packed with broad, generic terms that defy exact definition in the year 2010, words that good lawyers would call "weasel words."

Not only has society changed radically in two centuries, but every lexicographer and semanticist knows that even words change their meaning over time, often in one or two generations (need I cite more than the word "gay"?). Even a smart high school kid can find language in the Constitution so broad or vague that, as my Constitutional Law professor said, "You could drive a truck through it."

I wish they still taught Civics in every high school. Any good Civics teacher could have a picnic asking bright students to define:

"*Due process* of law"
"*Cruel and unusual* punishment"
"*Unreasonable* Searches and Seizures"
"*Excessive* bail"
"*Appropriate* legislation"
"*Good* behavior", and
"*A well-regulated militia*"

And any bright student would quickly perceive that judges have broad semantic latitude in interpreting many clauses in the Constitution in the context of current society, not to mention their own political and social philosophies.

If the Constitution is written in stone, as "strict constructionists" seem to believe, how can they explain the fact that most important decisions of the modern Supreme Court are 5-4 votes, and that canny constitutional lawyers can usually predict where a given Justice will land? How can there be a "conservative wing" and a "liberal wing," predictably and diametrically opposed in applying any given phraseology of the stone tablet? Why is it that a Bush appointee like Roberts can always be relied on to support the conservative position, while a Clinton appointee like Breyer will usually please the

Democratic side of Congress? Why was Bush v. Gore decided in favor of Bush by five judges appointed by Republican presidents?

The answer is obvious. The Constitution is a well-intended, revered, and semantically spongy set of rules for a highly evolved, highly complex society over two centuries later. And, with a few exceptions like Earl Warren and Anthony Kennedy, it will be applied by political appointees, albeit respected lawyers, exactly in line with the social, political, and economic philosophy of the President appointing them and/or his political party. Anyone who claims, or believes, that judges are apolitical sages who merely follow "The Constitution" and "The Law" knows very little about either.

The Supreme Court decision in the 2009 Citizens United case, holding (5-4) that corporations have the same First Amendment—therefore political —rights as individual citizens, overturned a century of constitutional law and should have convinced any Constitution fan that the Supreme Court, populated by political appointees, is almost as political as the other two branches of government, and that the Constitution is a revered, sacred semantic sieve....

9/15/10

Chapter 2

The Last Great American Freebie

T<small>HE NEXT TIME YOU'RE IN A FAST FOOD</small> or buffet or snack bar environment, take a look around. What do you see on the floor and on the vacated tables? Yes, maybe a few scraps of food, or food dishes. But without fail—napkins. A few dirty napkins, but mostly clean napkins, unused napkins, bunches of napkins.

Napkins are the one earmark of American casual eating on the run. They are the primary eatery litter, the last things bus boys and janitors pick up, and a notable ingredient in landfills. They are one item no casual, dash and dine eater neglects to gather. And they are the one item opportunistic, cost-conscious customers often collect and carry with them to cars, condos, mobile homes, and campsites (especially homeless sites).

Why is the paper napkin so popular? The answer is simplicity itself. Because they're free and because there is no limit on the number any customer can grab. And grab they do: I've seen some members of the proletariat, usually female, grab several inches of napkins—obviously for private use later. What else can they gather that's free, lightweight, and useful, where no one will notice, or care, or stop them? No, the paper napkin is the last useful freebie available to a hardscrabble American public that is watching every penny in a stubborn recession.

The question is, will the paper napkin bonanza last, or will it follow the path of the once-universal glass of water that accompanied even casual meals? Restaurants and food servers long ago realized the service and labor cost of water glasses with meals, or the cost of paper cup litter. Goodbye water with meals (and hello more profit from soft drinks …). So when will management in the food service business take note of the rising cost of napkins—paper pulp, remember—and start passing out one napkin per order?

Maybe not soon. Eaters love napkins and poor people love napkins. Most customers would be satisfied with one paper napkin. Some would ask for extra. But a few would also notice the switch and grouse about the demise of the last great American freebie....

9/14/10

Chapter 3

The Merck Manual Miracle

The Merck Manual is a compendium of medical maladies for general public consumption, a handy home guide that might substitute for, or lead to, a visit to a doctor. The latest edition contains 1,509 pages of symptoms, diagrams, and courses of treatment. It gives a hint of the complexity of the human body and the endless array of ways it can malfunction.

But the Merck Manual is an abbreviated look at the tip of the iceberg. Bear in mind that for four long years the medical student focuses on the intricacies and delicacy of the human body, from fetus to cadaver, and then isn't a physician until spending a year in clinical practice—internship. Then the physician may go on— up to four, occasionally five, more years of specialized training in one of the myriad fields of medical specialty. The fully trained medical specialist is therefore in his late twenties or early thirties before taking Board examinations in his specialty (becoming "Board Certified").

After the physician has spent up to ten years of

his young life learning how complex and intricate the human body is, and how many thousand ways it can malfunction or fail, he or she must wonder what chance a human being has of enjoying a protracted period of glowing good health, with all systems functioning perfectly and in harmony with each other. How long, and how often, can the nervous system, the digestive system, the skeletal system, the endocrine system, the pulmonary system, the genitourinary system, the circulatory system, the muscular system, and the immune system purr along in benign harmony, like a flawless Swiss watch or a perfectly tuned engine?

In other words, how many Merck Manual marvels are beaming brightly among us? I would guess that the Vegas odds of benign homeostasis would be sixty or seventy to one against it, about the odds of a dark horse winning the Kentucky Derby—and that's if the marvel is 20 or 30 years old. As the human body suffers the ravages of wear and tear, why wouldn't the odds of perfect health approach those of winning the California Lottery or The Publishers Sweepstakes?

A model of the Merck Manual Miracle would have to be a teenager without acne or asthma, a young athlete with no history of fractures, a Generation Xer with no history of appendicitis, a quadragenarian without a sign of GERD, a quinquagenarian without presbyopia (and therefore reading glasses), a sexagenarian without at least one arthroplasty, a septuagenarian without cataracts or diverticulosis, an octogenarian without crippling arthritis, a nonagenarian without macular degeneration, and a centenarian without necropsy....

I'm sure there are some of these medical marvels in our midst but, judging by the moans and groans—and medications and surgeries—recounted by our contemporaries in their "organ recitals," we don't know who they are.

7/12/08

Chapter 4

"Best By"....

SOONER OR LATER IN LIFE every human being comes to the jarring realization that nothing lasts forever. Nothing.

Not even landscapes or climate or cultures. Now they tell us that even the waterfalls and geysers and canyons in Yellowstone and Glacier are geologically temporary, here just for a chapter in geological history. If you watch enough *Nova*, especially in fields like geology, anthropology, and meteorology, you'll get the impression that not only are we here for the blink of an eye historically, but that the mountain ranges and ocean levels and catalogued flora and fauna are all transitory, ephemeral, temporary, evanescent—everything but fixed and permanent. Like the rules in a contest, or the terms of your credit card contract, or the latest airline schedule, everything you live by is *subject to change*—with or without notice.

It isn't enough to realize that our own personal existence has an expiration date, often rapidly approaching. Now everything around us has a similar date—medications, foodstuffs, chemicals, coupons, and marketing offers. Check the fine print. Most products in your supermarket and pharmacy have a "shelf life"— meaning a marketing form of expiration date. But the latest variation on expiration date and shelf life is the "best by" device, a hedge in food marketing against automatic discard or shelf removal, and also against complaints of staleness or degeneration.

The motivation for the "best by" hedge was protection of manufacturers and marketers against claims of contamination and deleteriousness if a prescribed shelf life or expiration date is passed. In short, the quality is guaranteed to the "best by" date, but you're on your own if your marketer is still selling it later.

I have to add a legal note here, a point that I'm sure will come up sooner or later. The Uniform Commercial Code legislation on the books in most states provides, for most marketed products, an implied warranty of fitness for the intended purpose. The lawyer for the sick or injured plaintiff will argue that the statutory warranty overrides the "best by" hedge added by the manufacturer. Or, in the alternative, that the plaintiff never saw the subtle "best by" labeling.

So, since everything around us is time-dated, due to expire, or "best by", the question is, what is *our* "best by" date—the Twenties. The Thirties, the Forties? The Fifties? That's debatable, and very individual.

As for our expiration date, that's also individual, but not debatable. And, fortunately, it's not marked anywhere, not even in the fine print. ...

Chapter 5

ENTRANCE REQUIREMENTS
FOR RETIREMENT?

THERE ARE QUALIFICATIONS EVEN for a successful retirement. There aren't any tests or interviews for it, and few people know what they are—other than a nest egg and some kind of monthly payment. Worries about securing cash flow and net worth eclipse the other prerequisites for a pleasant last chapter.

True enough, financial status is a prime factor in retirement peace of mind. It's hard to have a good time when you're concerned about sliding into silver-haired poverty. Insolvency is especially worrisome when you're gone from the labor market and your borrowing power is extinct. Lacking a sympathetic or guilt-ridden family, an impecunious retiree is a sad specimen.

But let's look at the tiger who laid away some real net worth, has annuities, a plump 401k, a nice pension, and/or some dandy dividends. His or her Social Security check may be pocket money or the mortgage on a second home. What else could that Golden Oldie need?

I'll tell you what. A few activities that are more enjoyable than the job was at the end. A sharp mind and a reasonably healthy body. And, probably more important than all of it except the finances, an innate self-esteem, developed early and never wavering.

Throw in a creeping realization that the world is such a big (and endangered) place that the job may have been a necessary source of diversion and income but was not a game-changer in the grand scheme of things. In short, for a sanguine retirement, add a serving of detachment perspective to the mix.

But once the retiree realizes that he or she is no longer a player in the arena, and is really just a spectator in the stands, the inherent sense of self-worth becomes the psychological mainstay, and the non-occupational friends and pursuits become the source of contentment, if not pleasure. Lacking the healthy dose of ego and a vital interest in non-occupational pastimes, physical or intellectual, I'm sure retirement can be a forlorn, self-pitying wait-for-the-end that could squander the bounty of the prime years, and be depressing for everyone involved.

Of course, this assumes that someone else *is* involved. An oldster who outlives all of his friends and associates, and who has no family in view, can be a sad specimen, with or without financial foundation.

4/28/10

Chapter 6

The Trust Imperative

O CCASIONALLY YOU ARE ASKED if you trust some-one. The implication is that you have the option to trust or distrust the individual, and to act accordingly. But all through our daily lives we find ourselves in a position of mandatory trust—of oncoming drivers, food servers, drug manufacturers, bankers, doctors, nurses, and airline pilots. Not only our safety and our health, but our very lives are in the hands of people we hardly know—or have never met.

People we don't ever see make our cars, prepare our food, fabricate our drugs, operate opposing trains, repair our brakes, and control the air traffic around us. Our only options are to trust that they won't endanger us—or to spend our lives in constant apprehension, paranoia, and neurosis. In order to function, to focus on our own pursuits and enjoy a fair degree of equanimity, we simply assume that hundreds of people directly affecting our health and safety 1) mean us no harm, and 2) are reasonably competent at their jobs.

The most obvious example is the trust of a patient entering anesthesia that the surgeon(s)and nurses know exactly what they are doing and intend to be extremely careful. We may have met the surgeon only two or three times, and know nothing about his background or psyche, but we are simply and clearly required to trust him completely as we lie unconscious and/or helpless.

Less obvious examples are the pharmacy tech filling our prescription vial and the air traffic controller or railroad computer operator who prevents a violent collision. We trust without even thinking about it, just as we trust hundreds of oncoming drivers not to cross over the center line and annihilate us at high speed. We trust because, to go on living in a crowded and complex society, we simply have to. And we do it without even realizing it—while still checking the pills occasionally and keeping an eye on oncoming traffic.

We are rarely betrayed in our mandatory, perfunctory trust. Amazingly, despite the distressingly low skill and alertness level of great portions of the general public, our trust is usually justified, and it's only in personal relationships that our trust and illusions are violated. Marital vows and fiduciary relationships are frequently breached, resulting in emotional pain and financial loss. But not loss of life or limb.

Better to lose faith or assets to someone we know and trust than life or limb to a trusted stranger we've never met. How ironical that, for the most part, our trust in strangers involves more real risk than our trust in those we deal with face to face....

8/04/06

Chapter 7

Even One "G" Is Giving
Me Trouble....

WE WOULD HAVE A real mess if objects having mass weren't affected by gravitational pull. You've seen the goofy state of weightlessness in space training.

So one G of gravitational force keeps the whole scene together here where we live, in the troposphere. With it we have control over our bodies and our property, traction for movement, even the oxygen we need to breathe. Oxygen has mass, too, so hangs around in the troposphere and megosphere. Gravity, bless its soul, keeps everything in place and under control at ground level.

But much as I appreciate it, I have a couple of problems with gravity after relying on it for eighty plus years. It seems that too many objects I am dealing with fall down a lot. Either I don't get a good grip on them or I fumble or jostle them. Or they simply slide off the place where I put them, thanks to a subtle slope. I have come to curse the constantly falling objects—something Maralys can't comprehend from an individual regarded as bright. And I blame the curse on a malady once called "the dropsy," although that whimsical term technically referred to an unrelated medical affliction.

Then there's this matter of skin. Skin, of course, has mass; in fact, they claim it's the heaviest "organ" in the human body … (I would have guessed the liver). Well if you grow to be quite large, due to a soft life, a vigorous appetite, or a glandular problem, you grow a large skin to cover you head to foot.

Then, if you change your lifestyle, or come on hard times, your body gets smaller—but your skin doesn't. It merely becomes looser, and starts to wrinkle, sag, and gather here and there, thanks to the unyielding pull of one G of gravitational force … In females and still-portly men, cushions of skeletal fat and mammary tissue yield to gravity, along with loose or excess skin. Do the terms facelift, breast implants, tummy tuck, and liposuction come to mind?

Having lost 30 plus pounds since retirement, I know whereof I speak. A thinner face is a good move, but there's this extra skin I developed 20 or 30 years ago and gravity has gathered it beneath my mandible, where it's doing me no good at all. No amount of facial mobility or massage will displace it. The extra flesh awaits a surgeon's scalpel and sutures if I am to resume my matinée idol role.

I blame gravity for this cosmetic insult—rather than the decades of gustatory excess that created it. Were it not for gravity, my facial skin would have remained in place, just a lot looser. Just another example of how gravity is slowly but surely dragging us down.

8/28/09

Chapter 8

On Buggy Whips and Cassette Tapes

MY DAD WAS BORN AT THE TURN of the 20th century, meaning he was old enough to own a buggy whip and see gaslights along muddy streets. My mother was a Flapper who, as a young woman, owned a few boas, and even into advanced age wore girdles. I used a slide rule in college and still own it; calculators were then heavy machines in offices.

Both my grandmother and parents played their phonograph records at 78 rpm with steel needles. I still have some of them, along with hundreds of LPs and neat little albums of 45s from the Fifties and Sixties.

Then, in the Seventies, along came cassette tapes and the Sony Walkman and boom boxes with tape players and tape recorders. Wow. What convenience and what fidelity. Name a classic and I'll pull it out of my tiers of neat, compact little cassette tapes.

Just don't try to buy a high fidelity player for the 78s. 45s. LP's, or cassette tapes. They were all replaced by laser-cut compact discs about 30 years ago, so now we have our classics on hundreds of scratch-free, tape-less plastic discs, just 4-1/2 inches wide, cardboard thin, and 20 to the pound. Wow. Keep them out of the heat and they'll laser-play flawlessly forever.

But wait, what's this about closeout sales of CDs in the few remaining (ex-Tower and ex-Virgin) music stores? Can it be that the CD is soon to be a relic, replaced by ipods and iphones and iwhatevers attached to tiny little earphones or perched in your car?

Apparently so, but guess what. This time I'm going to hang on for a few years, or a lifetime, playing my CDs as often (or as loud), as I please—as long as Maralys isn't around—until my last CD player breaks down. By then the iPods and iPhones will be on the electronic junk pile and our great grandkids (five of them already …) will be fingering a miniscule wire-less transponder in their shirt pockets—if they aren't already deaf from pharmaceutical ototoxicity or ampli-fier overkill.…

7/7/09

Chapter 9

LIFE IS A CASINO WITH NO ODDS POSTED

WE SHOULD ALL BE GIVEN honorary memberships in Gamblers Anonymous. Why? Because every major aspect of our lives, from the time, place, and genetic legacy at our birth, to the time, place, and cause of our death is governed by chance and by odds over which we have no control. And although we believe we make our own way in life through our personal character traits and a rational decision-making process, the fact is that most of our life-altering events were determined completely by chance, by luck, by accident, or by destiny.

For decades the sociologists and psychologists debated the relative effects of genetics versus environment as primary psychological determinants—nature vs. nurture—and although the geneticists may be prevailing lately, thanks to the genome revolution, either way the odds were set largely beyond our control.

We not only didn't pick our parents, and therefore our genetic code; as children we had little influence over where we lived or which socioeconomic class we grew up in. Our companions were determined by our neighborhood and schools. Our church, if any, was selected by our parents. Our sports were influenced by locale, climate, and social class, none of which we controlled, and by our genetic physical attributes. And our academic activities were determined, at least through high school, by our public or private school curricula.

Until we went to college, or otherwise left home, almost all the life-altering decisions were made by parents, neighborhood, or society. Most were affected by our genetic personal qualities and talents, but almost all, in reality, were beyond our control.

The course we chose in college and then in a career was superficially an exercise in free will, but both were extensions of genetic and environmental influences. A career might follow early personal preference, but more often is determined by family tradition or test scores, advisor or counselor influence, or just plain job opportunities. The identity and location of your employers are largely random or accidental. Job mobility is now the norm, and job sequence is essentially accidental.

In this and most modern societies the choice of a mate is the next major product of happenstance, hopefully a happy accident. The uncontrolled and unpredictable nature of the encounter inspires the traditional inquiry, "How did you two meet?" Although "planned parenthood" is a western goal, planned marriage is a scorned antiquity. "Love at first sight" describes a happy accident, not a predestined affair. And many, if not most, "blessed events" are anything but carefully scheduled events.

Likewise, no one plans, schedules, or can predict medical afflictions or accidents, whether acute, chronic, or terminal. Genetic medical susceptibility can now be determined somewhat mathematically, but most maladies and trauma strike on the blind side, including the terminal event.

All the insurance actuaries can do—until life and medical insurance can be written based on personal family and medical history and the personal genomic code—is figure the odds of illness or death based on large group statistics. That is a real crap-shoot, but the insurance companies cover their risks by shading the odds in their favor and by building reserves from a large pool. The secret is the large pool, endowing the insurance company with some of the aspects of a Ponzi scheme.

So from the setting of your genetic code to the assignment of your parents to the chance meeting of your spouse, to the genetic codes of your children, to the medical events that disable or kill you, your life is a fascinating series of uncontrolled, unpredictable, and random accidents that make it a complex, exciting, and hopefully productive adventure.

You may not know it, but you are a player in a huge casino, a passenger on an uncontrolled train, and a member of a leaderless mob. You are playing the stock market without ever making a trade. All you can do is enjoy the game ... ride ... march ... and control some of the odds as best you can.

8/19/07

Chapter 10

MY BIG OLYMPIC SWIM RACE

FIRST OF ALL, YOU DON'T RECALL the Olympics ever being held in Tokyo.

Well, actually, it wasn't *the* Olympics. It was the U.S. Army Olympics—for the Pacific Theater of Operations. And it didn't get a lot of press. In fact, it got no TV coverage; there wasn't any TV in 1946 … And the press was occupied with the War Crimes trials in Nuremberg, the Marshall Plan, and other post-WW II happenings.

Since the war was over but the U.S. Army still had thousands of soldiers not yet repatriated from the Pacific, Special Services decided that the Pacific forces needed an athletic competition in Tokyo. Swim teams were organized in five regions—Japan, Korea, the Philippines, Guam, and Hawaii—and brought to Tokyo to stay at the Meiji Hotel in Shinanomachi and swim in the Olympic size (50 meters) pool in Meiji Park. The Meiji was a nice complex, apparently undamaged by American bombers, a short train ride from downtown

Tokyo, which featured a large Army PX, shops, dance halls, and even a concert hall.

How do I know all this?

I'll tell you, because it all played a memorable role in my young life. After four quarters at Stanford and Oregon State, where the Army started training me to be a civil engineer (… !) at age 17, I completed basic training at Camp Wolters and Camp Hood in Texas, then ended up in the army occupying Korea in 1946. Our base, Korea Base Command, at Pupyung, Korea, was a former Japanese Army facility, and I was fortunate enough to have a private room in a former Japanese officers' quarters, and to work as an aide to the Company Commander, Lt. Thomas A. Landis. I don't recall how or why, but I didn't attend reveille, had a phonograph and classical vinyl records in my room, and did some sort of work in the company office. Recreation consisted of trips to a certain dance hall in Bun Chung, a pleasurable section of Seoul, 20 miles east.

Korea was to send a swim team to Tokyo, and, fortunately for me, there was no swimming pool in Korea, to anyone's knowledge, and I claimed to have been a swimmer in high school. I neglected to mention that I never swam in a race.…

Lo and behold, I was a member of a small contingent headed for what turned out to be a delightful two weeks at the Meiji Hotel. I don't recall an officer escort or anyone claiming to be our coach.

But I do remember cute Japanese girls working at the hotel, shaves and trims at the Tokyo PX, cute Japanese girls working in the Ginza dance halls (a ticket per dance), and delightful performances of the Mikado by Special Services show biz professionals in a beautiful theater.

There was a trip to the beach at Yuigahama and the Buddha at Kamakura. And a visit to the War Crimes trials, where I saw Hideki Tojo sitting in the dock … But not enough time to get up to beautiful Kyoto and Nara.

Strangely enough, I don't remember much about swimming in the huge Meiji pool—except for the race itself. I was entered in the 300 individual medley—6 lengths with 3 strokes (free, breast, and back—no butterfly then). I had never swum an "indo"—or 300 meters of any stroke … With my myopic eyes, I couldn't see the other end of the pool. And after only dance hall training, I was in no shape to swim *any* race....

All I remember is that somehow I finished the 6 laps, but the race was long since finished and I couldn't get out of the pool by myself. I can't recall whether being helped out was comical or humiliating.

Another team member must have done better. The Korea team went home with 1 point. Hawaii handily won the meet. But we returned to Seoul with souvenirs and some good memories. What more could you ask?

9/21/11

*"Congress shall make no law ... abridging
the freedom of speech ... " (1791)*

Chapter 11

THE FIRST AMENDMENT
AND ROOT CANALS:
A Study in Relative Pain

A S A SURVIVOR OF A HANDFUL of root canals, I think
I know what discomfort feels like ... But the pain
of listening to the two ends of the political spectrum in
our Jeffersonian democracy can put a root canal episode
to shame.

The radical left doesn't have much to say these
days, except for wearisome screeds about marijuana and
gay rights and equal pay. But the conservative right
wing is loud, ferocious, well financed, and dedicated to
the defeat of Barack Obama and a Democratic majority
(ineffectual as it may be).

After eight years of Republican bungling and
laissez-faire incompetence, the neocons and radical
right are building a Maginot line of resistance to any
reform and regulation designed to revise the Bush and
Cheney free pass for corporate and financial America.
And their relentless campaign to blot out from memory

eight years of social, financial, and military blunders—Abstinence Only, the Iraq War, sub prime mortgages, derivatives, a comatose SEC, a war against abortion, and tax breaks for the wealthy—seems to be working. The combination of corporate money and anti-Obama passion seems to be successfully creating a political amnesia that threatens Democratic candidates just one year after Bush headed for the ranch and Cheney for Jackson Hole.

The First Amendment is the grist for the fact that the American voter and the media listen to the loudest voices, rather than the calmest sages with the clearest memories. Noise and clamor trump memory and quiet wisdom every time. And money buys noise, regardless of the (mistaken) notion that liberals dominate the media.

The First Amendment imposes no requirement that "free speech" be accurate, well reasoned, or even well intentioned. And the Bush Court recently decided that free speech, including election campaigns, can be financed by any source of money, large or small. The owners of corporations—individual shareholders — don't even have a right to approve the financing of corporate "free speech".

So fasten your seat belts. Any similarity between what you hear in the 2010 election campaigns and what really happened in the U.S. during the last ten years will be coincidental. Free speech will be anything except "free" in political campaigns. It *will* be free of fact checking, moderation, or criminal regulation. We can only hope that it won't be free of ordered response from cool heads and unprogrammed moderates.

The conventional wisdom is that a democracy thrives on a free, open, and unrestricted exchange of ideas and opinions. I suppose that's true, though I often wonder—whether we are really thriving and whether time will tell. (We are still young as a world power).

In the meanwhile, it's grating, if not truly painful, to listen to the Rush Limbaughs, Glen Becks, Lou Dobbs, Bill O'Reillys, Sarah Palins, and Republican House and Senate leaders if you have any memory at all of Hoover, Nixon, Reagan, and Bush.

Too bad Jefferson and his pals didn't insert a requirement in the First Amendment that any American speaking or writing publicly know something about what he or she is talking about … But how could any court ever resolve that issue?

01/31/10

Chapter 12

Going With The Flow:
Streams We Live By

Streams are useful in metaphors because they signify a flow, and a flow is a graceful vision. There is something basic, almost primordial, about a flow.

And for good reason. At least three basic processes in our life involve a flow. Most basic is the constant flow of blood through our bodies. If it stops for two minutes, we lose consciousness. Unless restored within minutes, life is over. The stream of blood offers a continuous supply of the oxygen that every mammal requires. The bloodstream is life's primal flow.

Another element essential to sustain life is dihydrogen oxide—pure water. It also flows, starting with drops or small streams—but in our homes we get it from faucets or bottles. (How rarely have I enjoyed the luxury of a high altitude mountain stream?). Like oxygen, we take water for granted. It's cheap and it's here. Without it we couldn't live longer than a couple of days.

The next basic ingredient in our lives that flows

isn't primal, or even essential to maintain life. It's electricity. The easiest way to comprehend how basic it is in our particular form of life is to have a power outage. Everyone does once in a while, and everyone should, because there is no other way to recognize how much of our life in American suburbia is supported by the flow of electricity from distant turbines and generators.

There's nothing like a power outage to make you appreciate the dozens of batteries installed all over our property—in clocks, flashlights, timers, radios, and computers. But when we have to reset or restart them, it reminds us how many appliances and devices rely on the silent, invisible flow of electricity.

People suffering sustained power outages because of natural disasters quickly appreciate how different life was in the cave or tepee or igloo—and still is in the underdeveloped areas of the globe far from our view. The next time you throw a light switch, turn on the heater or air conditioner, start the microwave, or even check an electric clock say a silent "Thanks" to Tesla and Edison and all the other electrical pioneers who brought this stream into your gifted life.

9/26/09

Chapter 13

Thanks for Nothing Libertarians

M Y COHORTS AND I have advanced to the age when discussion of most trends in American society begins with the letters "de," as in degradation, depletion, deterioration, degeneration, decline, deform, derail, and deranged. So at a recent discussion group confab, we challenged our chronic critics to cite some aspect of American society that falls in a category that would begin with the letters "en," as in enhanced, ennobled, endowed, enchanted, enthralled, enriched, enlivened, or enamored.

All is not lost. Almost all of the seventeen pundits could cite a bonanza, or at least a rainbow, in America 2007. I started out with air quality in Southern California, citing smog alerts and sore lungs in the Fifties and Sixties, especially when ushering UCLA games in the Coliseum or playing tennis in an acrid blue haze. Others cited the panoply—or is it an avalanche—of new drugs in our pharmacies, and the new "drive-by" surgical techniques. Others saw the

Internet as a gateway to a wider, brighter world. One felt that civil rights have blossomed, if not flourished. And another cited women's medical advances, while lamenting the recent setback by the Bush court.

In an age when large numbers of the population question the competence, if not the legitimacy, of governmental action, it was interesting to note how little of the social, economic, and environmental progress we recognized came about through individual initiative and personal morality and how much through political initiative and governmental action. The cleaner atmosphere would never have resulted from individual environmental morality, not a wedge of it. The air is cleaner almost exclusively because government required it, through the Air Quality Management Board and through Federal and State emission standards enacted by politicians, not moralists and libertarians. The catalytic converters and smokestack emissions controls were devised by industry out of political and legal necessity, not corporate altruism.

Pretty much the same situation obtains for civil rights and women's health prerogatives. To achieve new rules, lawyers went to the courts—governmental bodies with power—not to university classrooms, church assemblies, or town meetings.

True enough, human initiative and ingenuity have produced surgical innovation and pharmaceutical advances, helped along by the corporate profit motive.

But once again, governmental action, however fumbling and inadequate it may have been, has been our only safeguard against dangerous drugs, tainted food, and medical quackery. Where would we be without the Food and Drug Administration, the California Medical Board, the Department of Agriculture, and the Environmental Protection Agency? We would be flooded by E. coli and Enrons and mad cow disease and Vioxx's and acid rain and toxic waste dumps instead of merely distressed by occasional governmental lapses and incompetence.

The next time you run into a Libertarian or other form of anti-government, anti-regulation, anti-political advocate, ask about the Vehicle Code and other traffic laws. Irritating though they may be, would you be willing to wipe the books clear of traffic laws, redirect the police and CHP to fight non-vehicular crime, and rely completely on the competence and good intentions of the twenty million other drivers on California highways? I doubt it. No stop signs or red lights? Please....

I would ask any American voter fed up with political hypocrisy and governmental incompetence to picture our food, our drugs, our highways, our air, and our environment without the action of legislatures and courts—symbols and wielders of dreaded authority—to limit our "God-given freedoms." I'm afraid that some restriction of our individual liberty is the cost of even minimal safety in an increasingly complex society.

The question for the future is probably even gloomier for Libertarians and other shades of anarchism. It doesn't take much of a crystal ball to see vast increases in social and political stress as populations increase to the point where air, water, food, and space problems inflame hordes of underprivileged to the point of conflict, if not revolution.

The very governments that are taking no steps to curb population growth may be the first to collapse under fire. And guess who will be left holding the bag —or attacked as the rich kid on the block—as third world countries erupt in revolution and/or war? Because our current political leaders (and even hallowed philanthropists like Bill and Melinda Gates), refuse to take even non-coercive steps to limit population growth, the specter of political and social unrest looms large on the horizon, and conflict is only a question of when and where. And individual liberties will be in for a beating like we have never seen since the Inquisition.

So relish the personal liberties we enjoy today. And don't fret over the fact that our politicians and judges make a few (?) mistakes with some rules and regulations to protect us from ourselves and our self-absorbed fellow citizens.

5/1/07

Chapter 14

DOWNSIZING:
From Detergent to Heroes

I T ISN'T JUST YOUR BABY RUTH and Twix bars that
have shrunk inside their colorful wrappers. Without
changing the size of the container, countless manufacturers have subtly reduced their product either by
volume or by weight—a sly attempt to avoid raising
prices. Who reads the net weight or fluid ounce con-
tent on familiar packages? the manufacturers asked
themselves. How many customers would switch from
Folgers Coffee if they discovered a little less coffee in
the can?

Other manufacturers, e.g., detergent marketers,
motivated by the competition for shelf space, and
the cost of packaging and shipping, took a different
tack. They reduced the size of the container and its
net contents, but launched an advertising campaign
to announce that the new product was truly "new and
improved", specifically more potent per unit so therefore equal in value and effect. In other words, downsizing was under no circumstances to be confused with

downgrading or price-raising.

Far more dramatic and painful is the downsizing by corporations in response to the Bush economic crash of 2008 and 2009. There's no way to disguise that kind of downsizing because people's lives are derailed. So clearly the "Great Recession" has given downsizing a very nasty name.

But there's another kind of downsizing going on that may or may not be related to product or employment downsizing. It's a lot more subtle, because it involves values and attitudes. Even emotion. That downsizing involves the American public's concept of a "hero."

A hero in this society once consisted of a rare individual who faced and overcame great risks and odds that would have daunted an ordinary mortal, usually resulting in benefits or safety for those around him … a George Washington or Sergeant York or Audie Murphy or Florence Nightingale. Someone who got a ribbon hung around his or her neck, or a high office, or a place in history. No ordinary mortal could be a hero until and unless transformed by confronting extreme peril or challenge.

What a different USA in 2009. Scarcely a week goes by without a somber ceremonial, an honor guard, flags at half mast, a cortege, a laying of wreaths, a candlelight vigil, or a bagpipe playing Amazing Grace. A teenager dies on a high school football field. A fireman is killed by driving off an embankment during a wild-fire. A policeman is killed in a chase crash, or a drug arrest battle. A college coed is murdered.

At the endless wakes and vigils and ceremonials that occupy the media, ordinary citizens are eulogized as heroes and heroines, almost sainted, when the occasion was supposed to be a show of respect for, or a tribute to, a fellow human who may have died too soon. Being felled by accident may be tragic, but it is not praiseworthy, much less heroic.

Sorrow is understandable. Grief is natural. But let's save heroism for someone who challenged long odds or demonstrated rare valor and tenacity where ordinary mortals would have blanched. Let's give good people flowers and affection and gratitude. And let's save a place in history for real heroes.

9/15/09

Chapter 15

THE LAW OF UNINTENDED CONSEQUENCES: Manslaughter Instead of Murder?

IT'S VERY TRENDY THESE days in political commentary to speak of the Law of Unintended Consequences as a pitfall for ill-considered policy and legislation. The point is that you had better think through all of the possible ramifications before you etch a rule into stone. Indeed, how brilliant....

But too often what the Law of Unintended Consequences boils down to in our roiling democracy is a euphemism for the Law of Inadequate Intellect. It's a little like saying we should avoid committing manslaughter, not just outright murder....

But a person killed accidentally—unintentionally—through reckless or thoughtless activity is just as dead as a person killed with murderous intent. The unintended consequence merely lowers the penalty for the fatal act.

The unintended effects of ill-considered political

action or policies can be just as baneful as though crafted with draconian intent. Look, for example, at the rise in teenage pregnancies as a consequence of the silly Abstinence Only policy—which left teenagers without contraceptives because of unanticipated sex.

The antidote to the Law of Unintended Consequences is obviously the application of lucidity, perspicacity, and prescience, otherwise known as keen intellect. In other words, the Law of Adequate Intellect is the solution. Unfortunately, in a society where, in electing leaders, noses are counted instead of brains, and where keen intellect is in increasingly short supply, the Law of Adequate Intellect is regularly lost in the fog of political turmoil.

When a politician employs the Law of Adequate Intellect over a period of time, he is apt to be elevated to the status of Statesman....

2/12/10

Chapter 16

AMERICA'S RED CARPET:
Star-Gazing in La-La Land

FORBES RECENTLY COMPILED A gallery of the 100 leading "celebrities" in the U.S. The collection offers a jarring but consistent portrait of the culture we live in. It shows who the idols are, where the big money goes and, in the end, reveals the values of U.S. hoi polloi.

The group consists of 17 athletes, 34 movie and TV actors, 35 pop singers, various talk show hosts and other non-acting show biz types, four movie or TV producer/directors, three models, two fiction writers (Patterson and King), two loudmouth right wing broadcasters (Limbaugh and Beck), and one radical talk show clown (Stern). There are no professors, no doctors, no scientists, no classical actors or artists, no serious writers, no CSEOs, no government officials, no reformers, and no philanthropists.

In other words, the American public is fixed on entertainment, amusement, and diversion. Spectacles. Amuse me, excite me, distract me, dazzle me. Give me motion. Give me volume. Give me flash. The louder and the flashier the better. Lift me out of my humdrum existence. Blow away my stress.

If there's to be any progress or uplift in the American future, it will come from a far quieter, less affluent segment of this society that doesn't seek or attain celebrity. Educators, researchers, inventors, classical artists, journalists, surgeons, epidemiologists, social scientists, and even some venture capitalists don't enjoy eight figure incomes and public acclaim, or have much time for celebrities who do. They aren't into flash and sensationalism. They're interested in innovation, achievement, enlightenment, and improving the human condition or the state of the planet … Quietly. Without amps and flash bulbs and noisy fans. Forget the tumult and the shouting.

Forbes will never gather and rank the solid core of this society. It doesn't involve enough money, which is the grist for Forbes. But Forbes did do us a favor by illustrating where Main Street America focuses its attention and spends its time and money. Without meaning to, it exposed the superficial, flimsy layer of society that gets the most allegiance and attention. It proved once again that there really are two Americas. At least two....

7/13/10

Chapter 17

CALL HOME JOHN QUINCY ADAMS....

IN 1823 PRESIDENT JAMES MONROE accepted the advice of his Secretary of State, John Quincy Adams (his successor two years later). He announced The Monroe Doctrine, which became a keystone of American foreign policy for a hundred years. It warned European powers not to try to colonize any territory in the 'American Continents' (meaning both …) But it also promised that the U.S. would not meddle in the internal affairs of European countries.

Since the "world" in the early 19th century was considered to consist primarily of Europe and The New World, Monroe made no mention of Asia or Africa. They weren't yet political concerns of the U.S., although Africa became the source of American slaves and Caribbean colonization, then China became a source of manual labor in the American west.

The U.S. dominated the Twentieth century, at least the first half, and the only foreign incursion to threaten us was the 1962 Cuban missile fiasco. The

Americas were never attacked or invaded except for the 12/7/41 attack on Hawaii, a U.S. territory. We kept all hostilities overseas, in Europe and Asia—WW I, WW II, Korea, Vietnam, and Kuwait.

But the 21st century promises to be different, not because of the ICBMs we feared during the Cold War, but because of some ugly new factors:

1. We proved in Korea and Vietnam that the U.S. is not invincible;

2. we seemed to be a paper tiger in Iran, Venezuela, and North Korea;

3. we alienated much of the Arab world by an obvious partnership with Israel; and

4. we invaded and destroyed one Muslim country, Iraq, without justification, then waged an unsuccessful war in another—Afghanistan— and will ultimately abandon it.

Meanwhile, at home, two trends threaten to weaken the fabric of the faltering leader of The Free World—economic degradation and political polarization. While the U.S. spent hundreds of billions of dollars in Iraq and Afghanistan, first blasting, then attempting "nation-building," our national infrastructure frayed and the deficit rose, and working Americans were replaced by foreign outsourcing and internal cybernation. While teachers and police are downsized and pensions threatened with bankruptcy, roads, bridges, pipelines, utility grids, and all manner of infrastructure degrades....

The air traffic system is antiquated. Blackouts and water shortages are on the horizon. Tornados, hurricanes, and earthquakes make news. The steady deterioration of the infrastructure and the millions of homeless families and hungry U.S. kids don't.

Meanwhile, Washington ponders the "Arab Spring," the revolutions in Egypt, Libya, and Syria, the Somalia famine, the suicide bombers in Iraq, Afghanistan, Pakistan, and India, and the financial illness in Greece, Spain, and Ireland. Haiti had its hideous earthquake, Honshu its tsunami. Where's the next disaster?

Guess what! Maybe it's time America had a new Monroe Doctrine—only this time one that says America not only won't tolerate foreign invasion, but also won't get involved in discretionary foreign wars itself. The conditions inside this country dictate that we can no longer be either the bank or the policeman for the whole world. We aren't the rich kid on the block any more; our resources are indeed finite. No one has appointed us the world's "Humanitarian in Chief," or the Commissar of Democratic Nation Building....

If it's going to adhere to its credo as the land of opportunity and a society where kids bypass their parents, America needs a rapid and a radical Renaissance.

We had better focus our attention—and our resources —on *America's* problems, not out of selfishness, not out of patriotism, but out of sheer necessity....

American children need lunches and teachers, America's homeless need housing, America's poor need medical care, America's deranged need treatment, and America's slums need renewal. Not only charity begins at home; so do nurture and therapy and renewal.

And so does defense. At the risk of being labeled a latter-day isolationist in a shrinking world, I remind you that we haven't won a real foreign war in over 65 years and that our military is now perilously overextended, per our own generals. A redirection of American focus and resources should create Fortress America. There is plenty of logistical and structural renewal waiting for peacetime military talent (a la the pre-WW II CCC). And in the event of hostile foreign attack, it should be remembered that 21st century war can and will be conducted at long range, with missiles and manned or unmanned aircraft ... And in rooting out homegrown ideopsychotics (probably our greatest threat today).

America is in alarming decline, and has been for years. The mid-America electorate is reactionary and ideological (take a look at the election map; the coasts are blue and mid-America is red). The K-12 education system is second-rate, lagging behind numerous other countries. The plight of the poor is third world. The middle class is dwindling. The wealthy are acquisitive and effete. Congress is dysfunctional (as I predicted last Fall). The judiciary is politically anointed. Local government is lightweight and over extended. The Catholic Church is corrupt. Protestants are hemorrhaging and dispirited. The evangelicals are semi psychotic.

Years ago I worried about the nuclear risk and the inevitable dire effects of the population explosion. I don't waste energy worrying much any more, but I'm saddened to watch the American decline and realize that my ten grandchildren and seven great grandchildren will never know the America I grew up in or, lacking a new American revolution, an America that sets the standard for the world.

8/6/11

Chapter 18

DEATH IN SMALL STEPS:
Accommodating Forced Retreats in Pleasurable Activity

WHEN YOU GO TO The Vermont Country Store and it looks like an endless array of over-priced junk pawed over by a gawking gang of rubes, what is it? Are you just tired? Are you dispirited? Are you terminally jaded? Or is it really a mishmash of ersatz collectibles and nostalgic replicas, and are they really a collection of bucolic looky-loos?

The answer is yes, and both. It's all of the above. You really are jaded and cynical and world weary. And the American public really is a large collection of gulls and buffoons, with a sprinkling of genteel literati scattered here and there.

The challenge is to keep your growing cynicism a little short of utter contempt for the whole culture, because patent contempt will certainly tend to isolate you from the herd and minimize your chance of geriatric ease and contentment, which should be your reward for leaving the rat race.

The unease that comes from losing my old interest in browsing, shopping, and people-watching is minor compared to the discovery that a combination of decrepitude and disability has eliminated my ability to fish mountain streams. That is not only a major loss of youth. It's a loss of personal core. I spent a lot of solitary youth watching unwilling trout in Vermont streams and Sequoia National Park. The rewards of girls and music and tropical seas were later and far away.

Any fisherman knows the pleasure of coming upon an inviting mountain pool in sylvan isolation and trying to lure a beautiful trout out of obscurity. The rarity of the catch didn't diminish the appeal of the setting and the potential excitement. The only sound was the muffled gurgle of the stream. The only obstacle was the branches above water and the debris underwater that loved to engage your hook. An occasional lost hook and pesky mosquito was your only irritant. A specified deadline and the threat of nightfall were the only background concerns—and both were often swept aside.

What I discovered in Vermont this time is that stream fishing is too risky with my ambulatory disability and balance problem. I am probably forever consigned to dock and pond and boat fishing, if fishing at all. That might be somewhat enjoyable. Pleasant, maybe. But it misses the big picture. At least the picture of *my* youth.

But it's not the end of the world. Or even the end of things an 83-year-old arthritic can't plan on doing in futuro. I no longer actively lament the end of skiing Orion at Heavenly-Nevada. And I rarely get a chance to discover that I can no longer do justice to calypso on the dance floor.

But, as in all cases where you don't have a choice, the wise choice is to redirect your attention to old—or new—activities that produce satisfaction, if not outright pleasure. And to forget about the over-priced bric-a-brac, country bumpkins, luggage juggling, security shakedowns, and airline connections that are involved in any trip to a clear-running mountain stream. Getting there is no longer "half the fun." And getting around there is now a little too tough.

Onward to tropical villas, PBS, musical theater, NY Times crosswords, and one-on-one conversations with calm, reflective, non-partisans (if any can be found). As we said after Eric died in 1974 and Bobby died in 1977, life goes on … And as Tracy often observes after any controversy or disappointment, "Let's move on"….

7/2/10

Chapter 19

How Much Folklore is Flimflam?
Gods and Demons in our Database....

WE ARE CONSTANTLY FED KERNELS of information by people who seem to know what they're talking about. They dole out facts and opinions from a platform of plausible authority. And since they don't burden the revelation with "if, ands, or buts," we confidently store it away in our vault of special lore.

With tech savvy Americans spending more time at their computer screens than in personal conversation, the Internet has now replaced friends, neighbors, and repairmen as fountains of information—or misinformation—that seems plausible and good to know. In fact, the computer is the first source modern Americans turn to for answers to their questions, leaving the library, the encyclopedia, parents, doctors, and teachers in the dust.

The question is, how much of this data and lore is unimpeachable—set in stone—and how much is as deluded as flimflam that lasted for centuries, like the flat earth, the Greek and Roman gods, blood-letting, phrenology, voodoo, and rain dancing?

Especially questionable are pronouncements dished out to the young, like a warning that finger nail biting will surely cause appendicitis, swimming after eating will cause cramps and drowning, and toad pee will cause warts. I was a smart enough kid, but it took decades for me to discard those wives' tales.

Even as an adult, I believed one plumber who cautioned against putting citrus waste down the kitchen sink—I still strip the orange pulp off of the juicer parts before rinsing them—until another plumber suggested that occasionally we use our lemons to clean out the disposal.

And I can't believe the medical lore I overhear from mothers who get their diagnoses and treatment from the Internet. How many experts at the keyboard at Wikipedia and Google are Native American medicine men or West African voodoo priests in disguise? And at what point does an Internet addict become an unfit mother?

Maybe the fact I was born in Missouri makes me a little more "show me" than the average person. But if I live to be 100, I'm sure I'll find that even more of what I've been told and read since 1927 was flimflam and humbug.

Maybe e doesn't really equal mc2. Maybe cats don't have nine lives. Maybe deficits do matter. Maybe cell phones do cause brain cancer. And maybe the population explosion will spawn massive water wars and famine....

The sun *did* set on the British Empire. Smoking *did* cause lung cancer and vascular disease. The medical experts *did* repeal the eight-glasses-of-water-a-day rule. The Industrial Revolution *did* affect world climate and sea level. And political cowardice *is* causing impending pension collapse at all government levels....

So everything we believed in 1950, then in 2000, may not be true after all. I hope most of it was, though. I'd hate to find out that we've all been living an illusion, a big lie, under false pretenses, or on quicksand (pick your own metaphor ...). I've lost too much faith and confidence already....

7/22/11

Chapter 20

CORRELATION AND CAUSATION:
Vive le Difference!

D O THEY STILL TEACH LOGIC in college?? If they
don't, they had better bring it back. And soon.
Since 48 of the United States—excluding the two rus-
tics you might expect to balk*—have just agreed that
fourth graders should be able to read and understand
Charlotte's Web, and eighth graders should know the
difference between prose and poetry (!), I wish they
would also require that college freshmen learn the difference between correlation and causation.

You wouldn't believe the difference it would make
in this poor confused nation—in politics, in science,
and in law—if the average educated American would
learn that correlation or association between two factors is interesting and worth watching, but that they do
not establish cause and effect.

Several beautiful examples of the confusion, even
in educated circles, are being bandied about in popular
science discussion. Since vaccines containing thimerosal are administered to children shortly before they

reach the age when autism is diagnosed … and since the cause of autism has long remained a mystery, a few behavioral scientists have concluded that the mercury in thimerosal must be a neurotoxin causing autism in toddlers where it had not been previously observed. Lacking a smoking gun in neurological pathology, they decided that the time frame *correlation* between vaccination and early diagnosis of autism is enough proof of cause and effect. At least three Federal Courts have now rejected the contention and thrown out lawsuits, but the plaintiffs are undeterred by the cadre of neurologists who reject the theory.

Then there is a recent article in the International Journal of Cardiology linking poor oral hygiene with heart disease because a significant percentage of heart patients had oral health problems. But cooler heads have cautioned that the association of the two conditions fails to establish cause and effect, that the correlation is one of numerous correlations in the case of cardiopathology.

Now we have some behavioral scientists in the red hot field of Alzheimer's Syndrome contending that there is a cause and effect connection between having a "purpose in life" and the onset of Alzheimer's, because studies show that fewer people who are actively pursuing goals in their senior years develop the affliction than seniors who are depressed or directionless.

While there may well be a statistical correlation

between the onset of Alzheimer's and the goal-oriented activity of seniors, there is probably an equal or stronger correlation between senior activity and hereditary factors, economic status, educational level, nutrition, and environmental factors.

You can do wonderful things with correlation and association; when I was a graduate student in Psychology, I considered proving a link between smoking and lack of breast-feeding … and we established our own lovely correlation at home—six breast-fed kids and no smokers.....

But much as I loved the potential of fascinating statistical correlations in my Advanced Statistics course as a graduate student, I never abandoned the precept we followed in one of my favorite undergraduate courses, Advanced Logic (which ironically helped me get a Minor in Philosophy). The precept was, in effect, that correlation is kissing cousins but causation is parenthood. (I think I'll copyright that …).

If college kids today learn nothing more in their math and science classes than the distinction between correlation and causation, they will be several steps ahead in solving a few of the horrendous problems they will be facing with the mess that "The Greatest Generation" is leaving them in Politics, Finance, and Ecology....

3/15/10

* Texas and Alaska

Chapter 21

CAVEAT HOMINID!

BEWARE. CAUTION. FORE! MIND Your Head. Read Before Signing. Duck! Incoming. Safety First! Recognition of risk goes back centuries, at least to Roman times. Isn't that where caveat emptor came from?

Two millennia later, the doctrine seems to have expanded to Caveat Hominis!—human being beware. Beware of everything and everybody: it's a jungle out there and someone or something may hurt you. Your government or your security system or your safety goggles, immunizations, safety belt, air bags, helmets, Mace, purse pistol, or personal bodyguard will protect you. If they don't, your friendly lawyer will help you find someone who *should* have protected you—and should now pay you—and him or her—some money.

Risk is the Holy Grail of lawyers and the home turf of politicians, law enforcement, bankers, and financial advisers. It's something you manage well to have a good life. But it never goes away completely. And risk keeps lawyers busy, either warning clients against it or finding someone to blame if it isn't dodged.

Legal documents are obsessed with recitation and assignment of risk. In a prospectus or proxy statement the recitation of "risk factors" involved in a stock offering or a corporation's business may run 25 pages of fine print, enough to scare the prospective investor out of his wits—if he ever read it—and designed to protect the company if something goes wrong.

But a disappointed investor's attorney claims his client couldn't be expected to read all the caveats, or didn't understand all the legal mumbo jumbo, or had a reading disability….

So the battle goes on … the risks come to life, or are expanded by changing circumstances, or are mitigated. New risks develop, or are recognized through increased knowledge (e.g., global warming, microbe resistance to antibiotics, etc.).

Small risks can be controlled or mitigated. But the big "Risk Factors"—nuclear annihilation, drought, famine, plague, comet strike, earthquake, tsunami, and drastic climate upheaval—can't be controlled by contractual recitation and insurance policies and government bailout. So the only solution is to recognize and control the immediate risks involved in your life, forget about the others, and enjoy the bounty we seem to have in spite of all the risks. So we'll let the motto be *carpe diem* instead of *caveat hominis,* at least for now.

2/14/10

Chapter 22

THE LUGGAGE:
Aye, There's the Rub

I THINK THEY SHOULD invent a way to travel without luggage. I guess they already have, for Heads of State and show biz celebrities. I've never seen a President, a Prince, or a movie star carrying a suitcase, or even rolling one.

But the rest of us have what for me is a very big problem. Even after you have survived the challenge of getting good reservations and reasonably priced tickets, too much of a trip is now centered around luggage—starting with the initial packing at home. What will the weather be like? And how many dressy occasions? The limited capacity of the correct suitcases makes a long trip a clothing selection contest that only a pro can win.

Then there's deciding what can get through security, making sure the bags are properly tagged, and not over fifty pounds, and distinguishable on the carousels, and unlocked or TSA locked. Never mind whether your airline will charge you for checking more than one, or whether the counter agent put on the correct routing tags—or whether the bags will arrive when you do. Even with state-of-the-art bags and correct tagging, your luggage can become your biggest headache.

Then there's the loading of luggage into cars, vans, and taxis. When not rolling, the bags are heavy. They are unwieldy. If you have more than two people, one should be a muscular male with special skills in spatial engineering. A group without a skillful packer, coping with small vans and cars, is apt to end up with several vehicles, or with carry-ons balanced on their laps.

All of this assumes that your luggage arrives on the same plane that you do. If it doesn't, you have new problems—several of them. Once the other passengers have jerked their luggage off the carousel and left, and you are looking at the same remnants endlessly circling the empty cavern, you find your way to the tiny Lost Luggage office and experience little consolation in finding other losers there ahead of you. As you fill out the required form and describe the lost bag in engineering detail, you are faced with determining which baggage slip represents the missing piece. Back to the faithful luggage, to learn—by elimination—the missing number.

A half-hour after you start this process you receive no assurance that your bag will be delivered rapidly, if ever. We've had ski boots delivered to our home six months after replacing them and receiving a depreciated-value check. And we've had a very important suitcase delivered to Maralys at our friends' English farm two days after a careless Los Angeles oil company executive in London mistook it for his similar bag. (Beware of luggage that is generic in appearance ...)

Once you survive your first night away without a key piece of luggage, you have your next decision—whether to purchase replacement clothing or wait another day. Hopefully you had your critical personal articles in your carry-on bag. Depending on your scheduled activity, you may not have the option of waiting longer to replace. And you may have no idea how generous the airline will be in reimbursement weeks or months later. And you probably won't go to the trouble of retaining counsel to press a claim.

The possibilities of consequential or collateral damage from a lost suitcase are unlimited, so I suggest to you that travel these days boils down to a few simple rules:

1. Double tag your luggage;

2. Buy unique or uncommon suitcases or give your bags unusual or unique characteristics, like colored tape or straps;

3. Carry on anything very valuable or irreplaceable; and

4. Don't go unless you really have to, or really, really want to. Travel is quite a hassle now, even in First Class. You have to be a real pro to make it fun and exciting....

10/8/09

Chapter 23

THE UNEMPLOYMENT CHARADE:
Where's The Unemployability Index?

ECONOMISTS AND POLITICIANS LOVE to toss around figures, peppering their speeches with numbers they expect their audience to accept as gospel.

Numbers about the deficit, the national debt, the rate of inflation, the number of mortgage foreclosures, or jobs lost overseas, or the abundance of illegal aliens among us.

Whether it's a campaign speech, a newscast, an editorial, or a sermon, you can count on an offering of "facts and figures" to buttress the author's contentions. Any offering without statistics in 2011 would have to be classified as an Emersonian essay or an encyclical.

The latest favorite figure is the one for U.S. unemployment, a number that says something like one in ten Americans is unemployed and presumably looking for work.

Who are we kidding?

Of all the phantom figures leaned on by politicians, this one has to be the shakiest. Fewer than half of all Americans go to a job on a Monday morning.

Start with the first fourth of the population—infants, toddlers, and school kids, including full-time college students. Then add the tail end of the population, the seniors who don't work outside the home or have some project at home. Some of them might like to hold a job today because they aren't funded for retirement the way they expected to be. But they have a hard time getting hired.

Then, without raising too much feminine outrage, add up the stay-at-home moms and full time housewives who haven't yet had a job and filed for unemployment benefits. And don't overlook the several million vagrants, indigents, and homeless who don't even get into the statistics, census or otherwise.

Now let's turn to the ten or twelve per cent that the politicians and economists talk about as "unemployed." Apparently this is the number who go to the trouble of filing for unemployment benefits. Presumably they once had a job—do they have benefits for "never-yet-employed?"

I doubt it. I think you have to start with at least one job, then get fired or laid off.

Of course the numbers don't include the swelling numbers of underemployed—people who are working at a job far beneath their qualifications, such as fast food, janitorial, or clerical. Multitudes of college graduates are holding what they hope are temporary positions—if they can find work at all.

But what the numbers *do* include is what I would call the "unemployables," whose psyche or intelligence level is so shaky that any screening process would eliminate them. They may get hired once, then fired; they then become an unemployed statistic when they apply for unemployment benefits.

The next time you hear a pundit or a politico cite the unemployment statistics, ask yourself what percentage of that figure was employable and what portion was actually unemployable.....

There's no question that the financial meltdown and the global cheap labor market have decimated American jobs, especially in mortgage banking, construction, real estate sales, and rust belt manufacturing. But for every skilled white collar or blue collar unemployed, there is an unskilled or ineducable "unemployed" that will remain a statistic and a drain on society for the indefinite future. There might be some sort of low skills projects possible for them, but unless they are palpably handicapped and fit into an existing aid program—these are shrinking, too, in our toughening society—they probably don't vote and aren't a real concern for most politicians.

So beware of the heralded unemployment rate—and all other statistics bandied about by politicians and economists. They are as solid as castles in the sand.

7/1/11

Chapter 24

CASUAL, RHYMES WITH SCRUFFY

HAVE YOU SAT SOMEWHERE RECENTLY, somewhere like a County Fair, a mall, a Vegas casino, or even at Costco, watching the American public in motion? I challenge you to do it. Give it at least a half hour.

Unless you have a lucky day, a lot of the words that should come to mind begin with "s": scruffy, scroungy, scraggly, shaggy, sloppy, slovenly, and slipshod … However, you shouldn't rule out grubby and unkempt, even though they don't begin with "s."

The adjectives you won't think of are groomed, polished, and clean-cut. People deserving those labels don't seem to show up in public, except maybe in places like clubs, salons, theaters, and financial institutions (assuming there are such people).

The fact is that, at least in terms of public appearance, Americans have gone downhill, to seedy and tacky. Tee shirts have replaced dress shirts, jeans have replaced slacks, cargo pants have replaced dress shorts, and sandals or flip flops have replaced shoes. Americans now dress in public the same as they do in the garden, the garage, and the workshop, except that informal has gone a step or two further, from casual to sloppy—and often on to grunge.

I don't know how many showers they take these days, but they seem to avoid the barber almost completely and shave only parts of their faces and necks. They must get their clothes at Target and Wal-Mart and the shoes in sporting goods stores. In fact, the haberdashers and manufacturers of men's leather shoes must be joining the ranks of the buggy whip, suspender, tie pin, and shoelace manufacturers—in limbo.....

Maybe it's just me, here in casual, semi-tropical California, spending no time near Saks Fifth Avenue or Neiman Marcus, or even in Court or banks any more. Maybe I spend my time where retirees or vacationers hang out—not bankers, executives, and fashionistas.

But we do go to the theater and concert halls several dozen times a year, and sit in the front of American Airlines planes every month or two, and I find the range of dress there only one cut above the checkout line at Costco or the Visual Arts building at the County Fair. Maralys never stops noticing the percentage of males who wear jeans everywhere, and I never warm to the ubiquitous sandals and sneakers (though I rarely don leather dress shoes myself).

The long hair is a generational thing. The Beatles and the Hippies came along far too late for my taste, and I still think that Tarzan belongs in the jungle and Fabian is an arrested adolescent. Beards belong in the 19th century, before Gillette made shaving a pleasure; psychiatrists must surely have some unflattering theories about men who wear beards today.....

Climate probably has a lot to do with the loose clothing, but the face hair, tee shirts, flip flops, and generally unkempt appearance talk to me about a combination of laziness and financial decompression that are a bad sign of the times, very bad times.

Maybe the clean-cut kids of the post-war boom —KKK's we called them—are a relic of early TV and the past. But if I was a teen today and wanted to stand out from the crowd, I would abandon scruff and grunge like a bad habit, trick myself out in polo shirt, chinos, and deck shoes, enjoy Gillette's finest, get a WWII haircut, and see which girls like a KKK.....

Meanwhile, I'm sitting here in a tee shirt, Costco shorts, and Maralys' castoff LL Bean bedroom slippers, nevertheless musing, "Haberdashers, Groomers, and Barbers of the World, Unite—America is Going to the Dogs. ..."

7/23/10

Chapter 25

Memo to Barack:
Forget About Mars...

JUST ABOUT 40 YEARS ago, our discussion group dealt with the question, "Space Race or Space Farce?"

That was post-Sputnik and about the time men walked on the moon. The advocates of the space program hailed a flurry of scientific and technical breakthroughs that would emanate from the space experience. The skeptics, I among them, questioned the promise of practical fallout for earthlings and dubbed the growing NASA budget a childish mis-allocation of resources needed to solve planet Earth problems.

Now, tens of billions of U.S. dollars and several moon landings and planetary probes later, the same debate should take place, and may be occurring subliminally in Congress. The NASA budget has been trimmed to eliminate for the near future any further manned space travel and establishment of a lunar base for Mars launches.

The 2008-2009 "Great Recession" no doubt accounts for the current cutback in NASA funds, although I suspect that a lot of the public romance with the space program dissipated with a few accidents and loss of novelty. And the Obama administration must take a (quietly) dim view of spending billions of U.S. dollars on space travel with the crushing economic and geopolitical problems facing 2009 USA. It seems downright juvenile to spend billions on space projects while ten percent (plus) of Americans are unemployed, millions are losing their homes, Muslim radicals are tying up our military across the globe, and there are climatic, agricultural, and water crises on the horizon. To say nothing of Federal and State deficits that are mortgaging the American future.

With this country in crisis mode, planet Earth keening with environmental problems, and a billion Earthling children going to bed hungry, how can NASA activists, chafing to get us to Mars, be regarded as anything but retarded adolescents who read too many comic books as kids and still want to play Buck Rogers with grows-on-trees U.S. dollars? I'm trusting that Barack Obama is too smart and mature and focused to give the space cowboys even a few billion dollars until Planet Earth and USA are out of critical care.

And that won't be for quite a few years, or decades—if ever.

11/03/09

Chapter 26

With Age Comes Surgery

I F YOU ARE LUCKY enough to live a long time—in my case 82 years—you are going to get knocked out and go under the knife quite a few times. Of course, the knife these days may be a laser, a scope, or a robotic knife.

In any case, I hope the sedatives and anesthetic agents don't kill too many millions of brain cells, because my latest count of knockdowns is up to 25 ... and I may have missed one or two. The list doesn't include office excisions, aspirations or injections where I simply bit the silver bullet or looked at the other wall. Fortunately, Chris and Paul Beck are very good with large needles, and my dermatologist clears off lesions (including basal cell CA), with razors and liquid nitrogen.

In a typical year M. and I have office visits with orthopedists, dermatologists, endocrinologists, and rheumatologists probably 25 times each, not because we're hypochondriacal but because we're taking advantage of the highest standard of medical care in the world, right here, and we like to keep the machine in the best operating condition possible. (Of course, as I write this I'm on a walker and a PICC line (for Vancomycin), thanks to a hospital-acquired infection in my left knee two years ago....

Once I get the new hardware in my left knee this summer, maybe M. and I can go into a surgical dry spell. She's had two major surgeries herself since Fall—the most recent a transverse colectomy for adeno CA —but she's now in the pink and ready to cover ground. Her surgical list is much shorter than mine—she's never had a chain of kidney stones (just a chain of babies).

I've compiled my surgical chronology as an aid in completing future medical questionnaires—but even more as a sort of perverted trophy list....

6/17/09

Chapter 27

COME HOME, UNCLE SAM,
YOU'RE DRUNK

UNCLE SAM, PLEASE SOBER UP and call home. We need you here. The party's over and you are no longer an honored guest over there in Baghdad and Kabul and Caracas and Cairo and Tel Aviv and Karachi. They will gladly accept your donations of cash and weapons, but they are frankly a little tired of you.

And, Sam, you are no longer the only rich kid on the block. You've got competition, and these days some of the other party guests seem to be a little more popular than you are.

Besides, we need most of your billions of dollars here at home, and we need them now. Our water mains are leaking, our power grid needs a lot of work, our bridges are falling down, our air traffic control system is obsolete—dangerously obsolete—our highways are full of potholes, our border is a sieve for terrorists and drug runners, our ports are almost completely vulnerable to dirty bombs, our Coast Guard fleet has been trashed by outsourcing, our Medicare administration is penny-pinching, and our population below the poverty line is in distress.

Sam, we know that you like to be a shining source of light and bounty for the rest of the world, but we can no longer afford to be Santa Claus for the other six continents. And the biggest favor we could do for the roiling masses of the Third World and our putative friends in the Big Eight would be to start repairing and protecting the United States of America while we still can—before we have darkened our grandchildren's future with even more national debt. Even our compatriots in Europe and Asia who hold a lot of USA IOU's would welcome our turning our gross national product inward to strengthen and stabilize our fraying model of democracy and economic strength.

Your days as a combination of Santa Claus, Robin Hood, the Pied Piper, and the Life of the Party are over. Or had *better* be over, if America is to remain a beacon and a model for the rest of planet Earth. After WW II and during the next 50 years, we could afford to be Daddy Warbucks. But the bonanza is history. The mine is played out. The wells are no longer gushers. The shining house on the hill needs work.

Come on home, Sam. My grandkids are counting on you.

8/20/07

Chapter 28

BROTHELS WITHOUT BORDERS:
Bordellos Are Just Plan A

WEBSTER DEFINES A PROSTITUTE primarily as a human who sells sexual activity. The classic prostitute is a female fitting the title of whore, harlot, strumpet, trollop, or lady of the evening.

But watching TV commercials and listening to sleazy politicians and unctuous evangelists remind me that Webster doesn't limit a prostitute's efforts to sexual performance. The second definition includes the sale or offering of a person's artistic talent or moral integrity "for low or unworthy purposes", a surrender to base, corrupt, or low motives.

Are the fawning actress in a TV infomercial or the bought-and-paid-for politician in a critical campaign less tarnished than a woman who offers her body to a stranger for money?

Historically and theologically, apparently so—but I don't buy it. The harlot is selling her body and her attention for a short while at a price, but not trying to deceive anyone. The deceitful thespian and the duplicitous politician are employing duplicity and deception for a price, with every intention of misleading their audience about their product, or their integrity or intentions.

Both are selling something in America, the land of the free market and the big sale. But the harlot is selling only her body. The poser, the ham actor, the huckster, the spellbinder, the rabble-rouser, the pettifogger, and the political hack are all con men, pawning their integrity and forthrightness for pieces of silver and leaving their fans as victims of deceit.

The few prostitutes I've encountered—I deposed them, rather than patronizing them—seemed far less culpable to me than the legions of phonies and slimies I see daily on TV and in the press, beguiling or hoodwinking the public for personal gain or unholy causes. The harlot is compromising her body. The huckster is selling a piece of his soul.

7/12/11

Chapter 29

The Deadliest Dogma

BY FAR THE MOST DANGEROUS SEGMENT of the Americana conservative agenda is the so-called pro-life movement, which seeks to banish not only abortions but contraception and family planning counseling. This perverted mentality flies directly into the teeth of the single greatest threat to the welfare of future populations, namely, the population explosion. It also creates a horrific dilemma for the hundreds of millions of young females who can't avoid sex but are not ready to function as mothers.

In a world beset with all the problems of too many babies born to unready or unwilling mothers—welfare, child abuse, poverty, undeveloped potential— it would be hard to imagine a more fiendish and counterproductive political movement than this unsightly offspring of Catholic and Fundamentalist churches.

5/29/00

Chapter 30

God Save the Libertarians!

THE BASIC PREMISE OF the Libertarian catechism, and increasingly the Republican war cry, is that, left to their own devices, human beings will do the right thing, and whatever is best for society. That Utopian outlook either harks back to a more halcyon, simple time or turns a blind eye to the more base aspect of human nature that codes of morality—and laws—were devised to curb.

Centuries ago, religious cabals were formed to devise codes of conduct to inhibit the brutish side of the proletariat, the lapses that lead to murder, theft, rape, mayhem, plundering and the like. Edicts, manifestos, and commandments led to Constitutions ... then to codes, statutes, and ordinances, all designed to curb the dark side of human nature.

We progressed from the mandate of the ten commandments to the canons of the Roman Catholic Church to the Penal Code, the Civil Code, the Vehicle Code, and finally the bylaws of the local Homeowners

Association … As men devised ever new ways to cheat, injure, torment, or harass their neighbors, ruling elders devised more rules to inhibit and control them.

Density of population increased friction. Rules and regulations inspired loopholes for opportunists and scofflaws. Scofflaws and opportunists inspired more laws and regulations. And so it went until a rebellion rose up against all of the restriction and regulation, with cries of "Let freedom ring" and "The best governed people is the least governed people" and "The only road to prosperity is through free market principles." You know the screed.

Ah, yes, the Libertarians and Republicans would have us go back to Thoreau and Thomas Paine and Paul Revere. Instead of "The British are coming" it's now "The Liberals are Coming" or "The Democrats are coming."

But we certainly can't go back to Walden Pond, which is no doubt now either dried up or thoroughly contaminated. We can't go back to the Articles of Confederation or any other compact without teeth. Unfortunately we can't survive under Amish or Quaker or any other simplistic or utopian code of conduct, because, frankly folks, "it's a jungle out there," not safe for Pilgrims, Puritans, Quakers, Pacifists, or well-meaning Libertarians. The nation's prisons are overflowing with several million individuals who wouldn't or couldn't play by the rules. And they are outnumbered five to one by sharpsters operating through loopholes or lack of oversight (a la Madoff), who haven't yet been caught.

Yes, even Republicans, truculent as they often sound, wouldn't survive long in the regulation-free world they idealize and talk about. They need the street smarts and combat experience of Democrats to set up rules to protect them, even against themselves....

3/21/10

Chapter 31

"Remember Pearl Harbor": How Could I Forget?

DECEMBER 7 IS NO ORDINARY DAY of the year for me. That's because of where I was 63 years ago, and during the several weeks before that.

On December 7, 1941, I was 14 years old and a student at Iolani School for Boys in Nuuanu Valley, Honolulu. My dad was a naval officer assigned to the USS Vestal, a repair ship moored next to the USS Arizona at Ford Island, Pearl Harbor. Because of proximity, our family had only recently had dinner in the Officers Mess on the Arizona—then, after dinner, we'd seen a movie titled *They Met in Bombay* on the big deck. All I remember is that the movie starred Clark Gable and Carole Lombard and, from the wooden folding chairs, I could reach up and touch the 14-inch guns above my head.

We lived in a rented house at 1056 South Beretania Street in Honolulu. It was a large wooden structure surrounded by vegetation, sitting next door to a mortuary. We had lived there only a few months because that summer my mother and I had come over to Oahu from Long Beach.

My dad was at home on Saturday night, December 6, 1941. Early in the morning we were all awakened by a lot of noise outside. Radios were blaring and all traffic on Beretania was headed west, toward downtown and Pearl Harbor. The radios instructed all military personnel to return to their units immediately, by any means possible. The excitement was intense, and down toward Hickam and Pearl Harbor black smoke billowed into the sky. Hurrying to get to his ship, my dad got into uniform and caught a ride on Beretania Street. The radio told us that Hawaii was under attack by Japanese forces and that all civilians should stay put so that military forces could get to their stations.

I don't recall whether my father returned home that night, but he never reached the Vestal. The Arizona had blown up, hit by a 500 pound bomb that apparently struck the powder room. The Oklahoma, next to it, was capsized. Somehow the Vestal had gotten under way and, from out in the water, Captain Young gave orders to beach the ship.

My dad reached Pearl Harbor at or about the time of the second wave of Japanese planes from the carriers north of Oahu. He couldn't get to Ford Island and was near the dry docks when the three destroyers, the Cassin, the Downs, and the Shaw, exploded, deafening him. He never returned to the damaged Vestal and spent the next several years assigned to Shore Patrol duty in Honolulu.

I can't recall whether we spent Sunday night at the Beretania house, but someone in authority quickly advised us to move. They were bringing truckloads of coffins made from pine wood to the mortuary next door and stacking them outside. Armed sentries were posted nearby and rumors were rampant—about "prowlers," about Japanese parachutists allegedly seen above Manoa Valley, where Honolulu got much of its water supply, and about a possible invasion of Oahu. We were instructed to fill our bathtubs with water and to get flashlights because a blackout was ordered for the Hawaiian Islands.

My mother and I stayed with the family of my best friend, Albert Madsen, in the upper Manoa Valley. The blackout was strictly enforced; only one room in a house could have light, with the windows completely blocked out. Vehicle headlights were painted blue, to be visible for only a short distance. Every night we stayed glued to our radios, listening to war news. All of this plus the complete uncertainty of the next Japanese move made for an exciting, unforgettable few weeks. Military vehicles were everywhere. Within days there was barbed wire along the beaches, even Waikiki, so that I remember we had to find narrow passages and maneuver our surfboards through the wire.

The combination of the blackout excitement and

the feminine charms of Albert's blue-eyed, blond sister, Virginia, created a high risk to my virginity, especially since I slept alone on a porch ... but despite her apparent interest, my clumsiness saved the day.

The schools were closed for weeks, if not months. Somehow I found a job as a courier for the U.S. Army Engineers, who had taken over the beautiful campus of Iolani's private school rival, Punahou, in central Honolulu. All I remember about my several weeks at Punahou was that I made $1.00 an hour (!) as a courier, big money for a 14 year old, and that we had gas mask drills in a tent (with real gas ...). I also remember that Punahou had a beautiful organ in the auditorium that I didn't know how to play.

School had only just reopened when my mother and I were evacuated to the mainland. I was just starting back to school at Roosevelt High School when the order came; I don't know whether Iolani's reopening was delayed. This was two months before the critical victory at Midway in June, so the future of Hawaii was still uncertain and most military families were being evacuated. One night a bomb blast on Mount Tantalus had created some anxiety. I never heard an explanation, but I did go to the scene and I still have a piece of shrapnel that I dug up....

Our trip back to California was exciting in itself. We were on the SS Lurline, the Matson Line flagship, its white paint covered with wartime grey. It was loaded with military personnel and military family members, a far cry from our trip to Honolulu the previous summer on the SS Matsonia.

Sixty-three years later, three memories of that trip stand out. First, we had destroyer escort and the Lurline traveled in an irregular weaving pattern, apparently in an effort to make it a tougher target for a torpedo(!). In April 1942, the Navy still didn't know where the Japanese submarines might be lurking.

Second, we were required to wear a life vest at all times, and in those days the canvas-and-cork-block vests were anything but comfortable. But the strangest quirk of the voyage was being introduced to a young Lt. J.G. named Butch O'Hare, who seemed to be regarded as some sort of a hotshot Navy pilot. All I recall is that he was young, cocky, and apparently Irish....

It was not until some fifty years later that I ran across a bust in O'Hare Airport that told the story. That airport was named for Commander Butch O'Hare, one of Chicago's (and America's), most famous WW II aces; after many Japanese kills in the Pacific, he too, was killed in combat. The reason he was already a hero in April 1942, was that shortly after the war started he had shot down a number of Japanese planes attacking his ship, the U.S. Lexington. In fact, I later learned that in February 1942, his squadron on the Lexington had shot down 16 of the 18 Japanese planes that threatened the ship.

My mother and I proceeded from Los Angeles to Great Falls, Montana, where I ended up herding 84 cows and feeding giant trout at a fish hatchery. But that's another story.

2/18/05

Chapter 32

Yes, But What Do We Do About It?

MILLIONS ARE STARVING AND being worked to death in North Korea. Hundreds of thousands have been killed or exiled in Darfur. Millions have been slaughtered in Rwanda and Congo. The opposition disappears in Zimbabwe. Young women are beaten or sold into marriage or bondage in the Stan republics. Dissidents are jailed in Myanmar. Elections are rigged in Iran. Roadside bombers are rampant in Iraq and Afghanistan. Shall I go on?

We have plenty of politicians, commentators, and political activists calling our attention to carnage, pain, and misery all over the globe—and suggesting that something be done about it.

But if you get to the end of the diatribe, the plea, or the screed, what you *won't* find is a specific plan for action. Invade? Bomb? Blockade? Declare war? Storm the United Nations with a demand and deadline? Or just emote, commiserate, and stamp your feet?

There's the rub. Anyone can spot the carnage and

outrage perpetrated by evil humans in every hemisphere and every continent. There are new Hitlers and Stalins and Attilas in every new generation, and the righteous caregivers of the world will never have either enough will or armies to take them all on.

So what do we do, except empathize and commiserate? The only solution I can think of for a nation is to get *very* strong, including militarily, stay very strong, and set a good example. As for the individual, aside from joining the Peace Corps, UNESCO, or a missionary group, probably the only recourse is to vote right (not literally), aim some checks at the most effective preventive organizations, and live the way you wish everyone else would.

And it would be a good idea not to dwell excessively on the human misery depicted daily on TV and in the press. That will only give you a sense of the hopelessness of it all....

7/22/09

Chapter 33

AMERICA'S CARTOON CULTURE:
Arrested Adolescence
With a Globe in Crisis

AVATAR. SPIDERMAN. DISTRICT 8. An exploding video game industry. $106.5 million for a Picasso cartoon ("Nude, green leaves, & bust") ... Give me a break! Are we a nation of children and simpletons?

It's bad enough when a high school graduate basketball player makes $30 million a year. And a journeyman ex-Angel pitcher makes $16.5 million a year. But when comic books take over the movies and young adults spend most of their free time playing video games or texting/twittering gibberish in acronyms and monosyllables—and when newspapers and serious publications are on the endangered species list—I start worrying about the actual value of my common stocks and the clouded future of my grandchildren. (Well, actually, I *should* worry, but I'm really not much of a worrier ...).

The world has never faced such massive

environmental and economic threats, yet American arts and politics get goofier and goofier. And American teenagers get more and more immersed in their iPods and iPhones, and more and more divorced from serious conversation. Outside high school classrooms or a college campus—our last bastions of intellectual intercourse for the young—do young Americans ever realize what a grim economic and environmental horizon they face? I doubt it, and maybe just as well, because if they really could envision their future, they might get grumpy and give up hope too soon to prepare for it in some fashion.

Meanwhile their parents do feel the stress and see a gloomy future. Polls show a rise in gloom and doom among U.S. adults, and loss of faith in government and politics. Disillusionment has reached cynicism, if not anger. Is it any wonder that they turn to crackpots and rabblerousers in politics (color Palin and Tea Party), escape on TV (think *Lost* and *Survivor*), and fantasies at the movies (a la *Star Wars* to *Avatar*). Reality is just too grim for adults in distress or those who see too far ahead.

Just what you want in a Great Society... Disillusioned, angry adults and goofy, self-absorbed youth....

Should I sell all my stocks and move to the Caribbean (an island not too low in the water ...)? *Nah.* We need good medical care and good show biz nearby. Steel bands are great, but only once in awhile. And the hospitals in San Juan and Miami are too far away. So we'll overlook the texting kids, cellphoning females, and juvenile movies.

PBS, NPR, *Newsweek*, and musical theater to the rescue!

5/8/10

Chapter 34

THE "FREEDOM" KALEIDOSCOPE

WHEN SAMUEL JOHNSON SAID that patriotism is the last refuge of scoundrels, he put his finger on one conspicuous example of sickening hypocrisy. He should have lived long enough to see today's beaming, All-American, red-white-and-blue flag-wavers of the U.S. right wing. I'm sure he would add the caveat: Never trust a zealot who wraps himself in the flag.

I wonder what Johnson would have said today about another threadbare watchword in our hallowed American democracy: freedom. Would he see it as the panacea of a vibrant free society or the password for anarchists, nihilists, and slackers of every stripe? I doubt that the founders of New Hampshire had an anarchistic bent when they adopted their state motto, "Live free or die," but they failed to define "free" for the laggards of society, and they gave freedom a prime priority over responsibility, productivity, and social comity that modern militants readily seize upon in challenging the social and governmental order. In our day, hasn't "let freedom ring" become the shibboleth for as many miscreants and scofflaws as Patrick Henrys and Guy Fawkes.

Oh yes, "freedom" is the password for everyone from Libertarians to anarchists, and the rationale for conservative opposition to almost anything new or anything with a cost. Freedom is an American mantra. But before you buy any "freedom" elixir offered by the flag-waver or the aggrieved, I suggest you ask for a definition. They may be selling a "freedom" you don't really want....

7/16/09

Chapter 35

The "Priceless" Myth

They say "You can't put a price on that." This is the frequent offering of bleeding heart logic that is designed to stifle economic reality and rational analysis.

The latest example of this mush was a response to the observation that a near-bankrupt California can't afford the very high cost of a 20,000 gallon jumbo jet tanker for fighting fires. The commentator's response, typical, was that, "You can't put a price on saving lives and homes...."

The fact of the matter is that you can put a price on almost anything you want to talk about. There are a few areas of human experience that don't have an identifiable economic factor, but almost none that don't have a cost in one form or other—psychological, physiological, social, ecologic, political, or economic. The law of Cause and Effect has never been, and cannot be, repealed, and is the mother of the now-recognized Law of Unintended Consequences.

Yes, for God's sake, do put a price on it before you

decide to do it or buy it or vote for it. It may be a poor deal in the end. All you need is some IQ and a little time to divine the ramifications and "do the math". Too bad more of our politicians don't have that capacity.

7/5/09

Chapter 36

Toothy Grins Ad Nauseam:
How TV Ads Are Giving Smiling A Bad Name

I S IT JUST ME? Or are you, also, sick to death of grinning, beaming TV actors telling lies as they peddle products they know nothing about?

After an endless succession of fatuous smiling faces in typical American TV ads, I often wonder if I'll ever smile again. But then comes the Geico gecko or the Ally snookered kids and I know that out there in advertising land there's still hope.

But keep the remote or TIVO control handy because the average advertising hack still recruits vacuous pretty faces and grinning roobs for that down home testimonial or sleazy pitch. The average TV adman must assume —or maybe he knows—that the average TV watcher is a simpleton easily swayed by gloss and mock sincerity. Thank God for PBS, where they gently plead or discuss but hardly ever flash a toothy grin....

11/11/09

Chapter 37

GUESS WHO'S KILLING GOOD GOVERNMENT?

A LONG TIME AGO, A TV mogul named Newton Minot described network television as a vast wasteland. He was right then, and he would be right now, PBS being the only shining star on the airwaves.

But at least the Fourth Estate, through investigative journalism, was minding the store in the seats of government and the corporate boardrooms, while commercial television skimmed the surface of governance with the "news." Magazines, and especially newspapers, roamed the halls of government like refs at a basketball game, sniffing out corruption and conspiracy among the Teapot Dome players, the Cosa Nostra, Tammany Hall, the Pendergast machine, Nixon/Watergate, the Keating S&L slickers, the Bush WMD fraud, and the Enron scammers. Edmund Burke was right; all that's necessary for the triumph of evil is for good men to do nothing....

And nothing is what we will get in terms of corruption exposure if the newspapers shut down, if there are no more Bernsteins and Woodwards and Moyers smelling a rat and digging in. Investigative journalism requires two things—dedication and a budget. The dedication should be grounded in principles of good journalism and a healthy skepticism (lots of humans will cheat and steal if given the opportunity …). The budget requires a newspaper or journal with sufficient revenue from subscriptions and advertising to afford roving, suspicious reporters.

You may or may not have noticed that newspaper revenue is down and staffs are being trimmed sharply by new management. Large newspapers are being acquired by titans whose primary, and probably only, goal is a healthy bottom line and whose last goal would be policing the halls of government and corporate boardrooms (Rubert Murdoch and Sam Zell being prime examples). Because of draconian staff cuts and altered journalistic goals, editors at the *Los Angeles Time*s are coming and going like day laborers. Revenue is down because subscriptions are plummeting, and advertising revenue is geared directly to circulation. With few, if any, exceptions, the major periodicals are in severe distress and contracting their coverage in order to avoid the fate of *Life, Look*, and *Liberty* and innumerable magazines and journals since WW II.

Why the disturbing decline in newspaper circulation? I'll give you three guesses. Your first might be the pace and stress of modern American life, with less time available to sit and read for part of an hour. You would probably be right, although most well-equipped Americans spend a lot of time staring at monitors or computer screens. Newspaper and magazine time would have to be carved out of the rat race schedule of upwardly mobile Americans, a prime reading group.

The next guess might be an offshoot of the first, a mental impatience I would call the sound byte mentality. Books became condensed books. News programs evolved to shorter, faster squibs after a series of hooks. Newspaper stories trimmed the details and cut to the chase, trying to eliminate continuation to a later page. In this category, *USA Today*, America's McNewspaper, is Exhibit A. Serious discourse and debates found a home only on PBS and NPR. Comprehensive, literate news stories in "column one" and in the *Wall Street Journal* are an endangered species. Lecturers make their points not with prose but with graphs and Power Point outlines. Advertisers have 15 seconds to pique your interest. Time is money. Quick is good.

My choice for the death threat to investigative journalism and serious discourse is the supreme new medium, the Internet. It fits in perfectly with a demand for accessibility and speed. The tens of millions of Americans, young and old, hunched over their note-books and staring at their monitors have little time or patience left for newspapers and magazines. They are too busy catching their news squibs on line, with no subscription costs or papers to juggle. They are blogging. They are texting. If a question arises, they have Wikipedia and OED on line. They've got Power Point and sound bytes on any subject they want. It's instant. Accessible. And it's free.

THE INTERNET GENERATION WON'T be subscribing to newspapers and magazines. *Time* and *Newsweek* get ever thinner. Even the *New York Times* can't last forever, as the Baby Boomers die off or finish their computer classes. Print journalism is in mortal danger. Slowly but surely the Internet is killing it off.

Who will be left to sniff out the grafters, conspirators, defrauders, and other slimy characters in government offices and corporate boardrooms? The FBI? The CIA? The SEC? The FDA? The FCC? The Attorneys General? The District Attorneys?

Good luck, America. Don't hold your breath. Did any of them uncover the Teapot Dome Scandal? Or the Nixon scandal? The Keating scandal? The Enron scandal? The toy dangers? The food contamination? The dangerous pharmaceuticals?

Not really. Government agencies usually get involved after journalists and attorneys blow whistles. Like most politicians and government functionaries, they don't act; they react.

If the journalists fade away and the attorneys get shut down by more "conservative" judges, corrupt politicians and scheming captains of industry should have a field day. The texters and bloggers (and talk radio heads), may complain, castigate, even pontificate about them. But will they expose and unseat them through public outrage?

Not if they are just a million neighbors talking over the back fence. Not without the dirt uncovered by journalists hankering for a scoop or attorneys hungry for a kill. They're the story-sniffing bloodhounds who dig through records and interview people who know things.

Will e-mailers and bloggers and texters fill the investigative gap? Time will tell, but don't bet on it. When the last serious newspaper shuts down and the last *60 Minutes* program airs, this democracy is in big trouble.

3/08

Chapter 38

WHEN DID CONSERVATIVE BECOME A DIRTY WORD?

WITH ME, ABOUT 30 years ago. Because up until then I always thought I *was* one ... My family had been Republican from the start and we associated Democrats with labor unions, blue collar workers, strikes, and giveaway programs. My parents thought Roosevelt was a Socialist who pandered to the lower classes (even though my Dad admired the CCC program as a camp commander during the Depression). We thought Truman was a Missouri hick who had the nerve to recall a noble Douglas MacArthur. We thought Nixon was robbed by a Catholic slicker and I thought (until I met him) that Jimmie Carter was a Georgia hayseed ... and I called him Jimmy Peanut.

HOW THINGS CHANGED WHEN a charismatic former life guard and second-rate movie actor became the quintessential conservative and demonstrated how intellectually vacuous a Republican icon can be. Reagan belittled government while ballooning the defense budget—as the USSR was already crumbling from within. Like George W. Bush, he played the role of a fiscal conservative, cutting taxes while the national debt ballooned like never before (even during WW II).

In fact, the greatest indictment against the so-called conservative politicos is something their fans never seem to look at—the chart of the national debt that Republicans talk so much about. Since Dwight Eisenhower, the last good Republican president in my book, only Reagan and the two Bushes—twenty years of "conservative" leadership—have vastly increased the national debt by huge annual deficits. Teddy Roosevelt and Dwight Eisenhower and Bob Taft—all good Republicans—would be horrified to study the chart of the national debt versus the political posture of Reagan and the two Bushes.

Admittedly, the national deficit is out of control again, this time with Democrats in power, but the cause is two ridiculous George W. Bush wars and a near-Depression brought on by eight years of Republican deregulation and a decade of generic moral decline in the American financial community. Time will tell whether the new Republican House can bring back some fiscal conservatism without reviving a near-depression.

Another nasty habit of the neocons, starting with Reagan, also poorly publicized, is their antipathy toward social and environmental programs. Reagan was being his jolly self when he declared that if you've seen one redwood, you've seen them all. But his opinion that most of the homeless and mental hospital patients were alcoholics or lazy or shiftless caused grievous long term damage when the mental hospitals were all but shut down and the jail population mushroomed (thanks also to the law-and-order brand of conservatism). Again , an irony. One of California's critical deficit factors is the largest jail population in the country, a system totally out of control. Yet who have been the loudest segment of the third strike, throw-away-the-key crowd in the California courts and political process? You betcha— the conservative right wing of the Republican party.

Now the right wing is out to kill all funding for the National Endowment For The Arts, National Public Radio, the Americorps program, PBS, Planned Parenthood, and almost every other cultural or intellectual program as liberal profligacy—but actually as natural enemies of conservative politics. Name a program supported by governmental funding that is in any way favored by intellectuals and you will find "conservative" opposition and name-calling, whether by Tea Party dimwits, Sarah Palin, or right wing Republicans.

And you will also see why I now reject most conservative doctrine since Reagan ... as anti-intellectual, antisocial, anti-environmental, and Philistine. Not to mention outrageously hypocritical in any true accounting sense. And why one of my favorite appellations during my first 50 years is now a dirty word.

2/14/11

Chapter 39

The Back Road to Tyranny

T YRANNY IS SURELY ON your list of evils, although, as you fume in traffic and juggle your finances, you probably aren't dealing with it on a daily basis. It's just something you are supposed to hate if you become a victim. Think of Hitler, Stalin, and Ceauşescu.

I suspect we all suffer a few effects of tyranny, but only in a masked, indirect fashion. Students may consider responses of school administrators to certain behavior as tyrannical. Demonstrators often regard police response as tyrannical. Citizens cut off in public forums get a taste of tyranny. Small businesses battling City Hall may get a strong sense of tyranny. And political activists, starting with anarchists and libertarians, surely believe they are waging a battle against the forces of tyranny.

The average person's discomfort resulting from governmental action in Washington or Sacramento, or even local government bodies, is so muted that tyranny is not assigned blame. The culprit is regarded as incompetence or hysteria or desperation, not tyranny. Tyranny must be wreaked by an individual, not a deliberative body—or so it seems. A judge or a bureaucrat can be a tyrant, but a governing body is (simply) just misguided or shortsighted (if not corrupt).

Ask yourself, what forces create and guide a tyrant? Is it a psychological flaw, a deep-seated insecurity, a drive for recognition, an appetite for vengeance fueled by rage? Or is it an ideology, a distrust of associates, a conviction of superiority, an impatience with incompetence, or an ego out of control?

Whatever the cause, a tyrant harbors a contempt for communal action and the democratic process. And in the end he or she will usually be toppled, dethroned, and disgraced, if not executed. Few tyrants die at the summit of their power.

My focus here is the breeding ground for tyranny, its genesis. What makes a society fertile for oppression and over regulation?

I'm sure there are multiple causes, but let me offer two that you might not think of. The first is public immorality, ranging from the scofflaw to the misdemeanant to the felon. The fact that there are 2.4 million Americans in jail—the highest per capita rate in the civilized world—is a pretty good sign that society is mad as hell and won't take it any more ... Add to that the fact that most misdemeanants and felons don't get caught or, if arrested ... convicted. You are looking at some big numbers. And this doesn't include the percentage of the population that cheats or fudges in non-criminal ways, but who nevertheless increase the cost of government or products, or who reduce tax revenue.

Examples of public immorality (or amorality), are legion. Office and factory pilferage, not to mention embezzlement. Vandalism and graffiti. School cheating. Sundry under the table, unreported cash dealings.

The response of government: more regulation, higher tax rates, and more fees. Immorality costs money—and leads to regulation, a stepping stone on the road to oppression and tyranny.

The other breeding ground for government response is congestion, urban or otherwise. It causes friction, and friction causes conflict. Scattered conflicts result in lawsuits, but major conflicts lead to regulation.

The driving force of congestion is overpopulation, and overpopulation, unless there is a radical change in the Catholic Church and the current Federal administration, is here to stay. As resources become strained and social conflict escalates, the risk of harsh governmental action increases. Can oppression and tyranny be far behind?

I don't have the answer to blunting the risks created by public immorality and the population explosion. The solutions probably won't come through typical governmental action or political maneuvering. Perhaps they'll come from some charismatic or Messianic oracle(s) or from societal epiphany not yet visible on the horizon.

Meanwhile, bask in the generous and unparalleled measure of freedom that we still enjoy in the USA in 2007 and do what you can to preserve it.

7/3/07

Chapter 40

Open Season on Slander and Libel

There's always been a risk of venomous personal attack via a poison pen letter (signed or unsigned), or an anonymous note on a bulletin board or doorway. But today the angry, the jilted, the banished, and the deranged have a vastly more powerful weapon for a guerrilla hit and run attack.

Of course I'm referring to the Internet, where millions can vent their spleens or practice character assassination without even buying a 41-cent stamp or printing a diatribe. The blog is the assassin's new Stinger missile and the keyboard his automatic weapon....

Unless his target is George Bush, Dick Cheney, or the U.S. Government, he or she needn't worry about a visit from the FBI or the Secret Service, even if the blogger signs his name. And what civil or criminal recourse would be available to the victim against a judgment-proof blogger hunched over a keyboard in a dorm, walk-up, or other humble abode? You've got it. *Nada. Rien.* Zip.

Welcome to a Brave New blog-infected World, where a lethal virus can attack you from any direction—a virus against which you cannot get vaccination immunity. Is anyone out there offering reputation protection insurance?

3/31/08

Chapter 41

Storm Clouds on the Horizon

I F WE STEP BACK A LITTLE, we see some trends that are both sad and foreboding. The newspaper/magazine hemorrhage started several years ago, thanks to the Internet as a substitute information source and its devastating effect on print media circulation (which determines advertising revenue). How many Baby Boomers and Generation Yers do you know who read a newspaper and one or two news magazines? Not many. Hence the continuing decimation of newspaper staffs and trimming of newsprint volume.

A secondary consequence of newsprint hemorrhaging will be a surge in corporate and government corruption, as newspapers and news services exhaust their budgets for investigative journalism. The Woodwards, Bernsteins, and Moyers cost real money, more than routine reporters, and history reveals that it's investigative journalists patrolling the halls of government and corporate suites who smell and expose the rats. The government agencies and trial lawyers close in for the kill, like vultures, but rarely uncover the rats in the first place.

The increase in juvenile violence is also an obvious matter of concern. If you examine the blatant and incessant stream of violence they feed on in their video games and movies and comic books, you probably won't wonder about the cause. The disappearance of the traditional family home and the decline in religious influence obviously play a role. There is no turnaround on the horizon—and U.S. jails are already overflowing and threatening the solvency of state and local government.

Then there is the frenetic tempo of life in young America that only gets worse. Generation Y may not see itself turning into a horde of fluttery, twitchy sound byte texters and twitterers, but they are—victims of an epidemic of cultural Attention Deficit Disorder. Their attention is scattered by noise, and rapid-fire conversation on the fly. Their schedules are so full that they live life on the run.

Their music is loud and up tempo, heavy in percussion. Their TV is fast paced and fast talking. Lots of film clips and squibs.

Multi-tasking prevails: cell phone or texting while driving. Earphones while studying. Homework interspersed with phone calls, texting, or TV. Discussions short clipped and to the point. Cut to the chase. No time for rumination. (They don't even know the word). A life in short clips. And when it's over, the heyday at least, they probably won't even know what happened … It all went by so fast.…

While Generation Y texts and twitters its life away, Generation X is succumbing to another malady —compassion fatigue, led by the Tea Party hotshots and the Republican right wing. The new rebellion in Congress and the Statehouses reflects a growing impatience with out-of-control entitlements, protective regulations, and government programs in general.

The new patriot rebels harbor a true cynicism about the beneficiaries of social and welfare programs. They have no sympathy for those they regard as the millions of indolent and incapable losers in a free market … and in a financial crisis they reject the cost of carrying the luckless on the backs of the rich—a crisis brought about by preemptive foreign wars and, ironically, laissez-faire governmental policies.…

Ayn Rand is alive and well. In the delusion that less government is the solution, and that the law of the jungle is the true path out of our financial morass, Rand becomes the poster girl for the radical right.

In November 2012 we'll find out how feeble-minded the American electorate really is.…

6/6/11

Chapter 42

THE RVW ECONOMIC CREED

IF YOU DON'T GROW, EXTRACT, or fabricate something, you are completely dependent on the skills and largess of others, because every human needs food, shelter, clothing, and tools. Farmers, breeders, loggers, miners, builders, and manufacturers support us all.

If a society evolves to a point where only a small minority are actually producing food and hard goods, and a huge majority are basically consumers, spokesmen, spectators, and philosophers, hardship and fatal dependency are just around the corner....

11/24/07

Chapter 43

A Sudden Dose of Melancholy:
Death in Little Steps

A STARTLING REMINDER OF the transitory nature of life and its relationships comes with a review of an old phone directory or Christmas card address list. Noting the number of people who moved away, died, or otherwise dropped off the radar screen completely also creates a bit of a shock and is a little like a preview of your own demise. For whatever reason, you yourself have dropped off the screens of former neighbors, relatives, and good friends.

Likewise, a review of an old letter file or a school yearbook. Or a photo album. How can common paths branch off so completely that the Whatever Happened To list gets longer and longer? How many classmates and early friends are on that list? Where are they? Are they even alive on this planet? Do they remember me as someone unusual or special? Who broke the chain of communication first? Do they ever think of us? How could we have been so close and then broken off contact? Will the pattern continue?

IS THIS LIFE'S NATURAL course? Is death merely the final break in contact with everyone who loved or cared about you for a time?

The next time you update your address or phone directory, ask yourself, why the change? Is it because you dropped off their list, or they died, or you lost interest in them? Does familiarity always breed contempt? Or is novelty an attraction? If the person is still local, did he or she bore you, or irritate you, or merely drop you from his or her list?

How many other than immediate family will stay on your list to the end? Is your list getting longer or shorter? Do political or religious orientation play a role in changing affinity? Are blood and age the only common factors as time marches on?

Nostalgia is usually tinged with sadness because we lament the loss of something or someone dear. Gone and almost forgotten. But not quite. How did we let it all get away? Why can't we hang onto The Good Times? And the special (young) friends?

I wonder if we will have the same reaction when we update our address lists and phone directory ten years from now?

5/11/07

Chapter 44

THE APOSTASY CREED:
(With apologies to the Apostles' Creed)

1. Don't believe any story out of the Middle East, old or new, unless it's confirmed by film at eleven …

2. Immaculate conception was an explanation devised to protect the reputation of a young Jewish wife and to deter terrible humiliation of a baffled husband …

3. The drama and martyrdom of crucifixion was a godsend for the disciples of J.C., a huge P.R. bonanza …

4. The body-snatching maneuver of Christ's devotees sealed the myth … (remember the old gag telegram from Ben Gurian to the Pope: "Cancel Easter—we found the body" …

5. If Jesus Christ were alive today he would be a billionaire televangelist in Palm Springs and blow away all of his self-appointed spokesmen like Falwell and Robertson and James Dobson …

6. Religion's role is pure and simple: answer the unanswerable questions—why are we here and why do we die and where do we go?

7. You can fool most of the people most of the time if you sell a balm that allays their fears and offers them hope ...

11/24/07

Chapter 45

"NEVER AGAIN!": Transient Irritation Or Morbid Foreclosure?

THE NEXT TIME YOU ANNOUNCE, in a fit of frustration, "That's it—Never again," ask yourself exactly what you mean. If you are swearing off that person, or that place, or that activity, for the time being, you don't really mean "Never". Because never means never, not ever again, never in the course of human history. Meaning that that element in your life is foreclosed forever, blocked off, terminated.

In other words, that portion of your life just ended. Forever. Like you died to that extent. An early installment on death....

I think I'll switch to, "Not again, soon." I'd rather leave the door open a little, in case things change. I'm not ready to die yet. Not even a little bit.

7/10/09

Chapter 46

THINGS YOU CAN LEARN
IF YOU MAKE GIFTS

IF YOU LIVE LONG ENOUGH you learn some interesting things. Even things about taxes and gifts and grand-kids ... things that involve money, so are very important.

We have been giving stock (and cash) to grand-kids off and on for seven years, using some rather obscure legislation known as the California Uniform Gift to Minors Act. Federal tax law now allows gift-tax-free gifts of up to $12,000 per person, meaning a gift of $24,000 of community property by a California couple. That's per year. There is also a $1 million life-time limit for gift-tax-free gifts and I'll have to check one of these days to see whether the $12,000 annual gifts count toward that limit.

The Federal Gift tax is imposed on the donor, not the donee, so the limits are our worry, not the grand-kids'. Their tax exposure comes in a different way, when they sell the gifted stock (or other capital asset). If there is a capital gain involved, and if their passive income is over $700, or they have active income, they owe Federal (and maybe State) tax.

The question has arisen a few times now, when do they have a gain (or loss)? What is their tax basis for the gifted stock: is it our tax basis or the value at the time of the gift? And if we held the stock for decades, what is our basis? Was the stock purchased by us or acquired by gift, or by inheritance? If so, what was the tax basis of the donor if we were the donee, etc., etc. Trust me: it gets complicated and involves a lot of paperwork, or even correspondence. There are cases where the stock was acquired decades ago and the original purchaser is long since dead and records unavailable.

We purchased the bulk of our stock, a lot of it years ago, but I am a record keeper, as you know, so can dig out most purchase data. However, the picture gets even more complicated because of stock splits. Every time a company splits the stock, the tax basis changes. For example, if GE stock split three times in 10 years, twice at 2-for-1 and once at 3-for-1, your tax basis for those shares would be only one twelfth of the original cost. Try moving that back through a prior donor, or an inheritance (which moves the tax basis up to the time of death). Then figure in any subsequent purchase of GE stock and you have a real paperwork challenge.

That isn't the end of the problems...It isn't easy to unravel all of the stock splits you may have enjoyed over the years. The average investor doesn't have a clue, so must rely on a stock brokerage firm to dig it out.

My Standard and Poor's stock guide covers (in tiny footnotes) only splits in the last four years, so I have to dig out splits before 2003....

ONCE WE LEARNED THAT *our* tax basis is necessary if a grandkid sells stock, and I went through the above process a few times, I learned a very big lesson—a caution that I have never seen in the endless reading that I do in the business journals. It involves another nasty aspect of Federal tax law, namely, that any money or stock that you take out of your IRA is taxed at ordinary income rates—even though the stock may represent years of capital gain growth while in the IRA. And you may or may not know that after age 70 we are required to take money (or stock) out of an IRA every year, based on a formula, and increasing in percentage every year as we age....

The result of this rule (Minimum Required Distribution) is that, over the past 17 years, more than half of our annual tax bill represents my MRD from my IRA that did rather well (especially with medical and energy stocks.)

So, guess what. When stock is taken out of the IRA—and we pay ordinary income tax rate on its full value—the tax basis for that stock is immediately raised to the market value when we remove it—in other words, the value we pay the tax on. So that's the stock we should be giving as gifts, because if the grandkid sells it in the next few years, there will be a modest gain (or loss) in value, resulting in a much smaller capital gain to the grandchild, if there is a gain at all.

I learned this crucial lesson recently, when grand-kids sold both some "old" stock that wasn't in my IRA and some stock I had recently taken out of the IRA as part of a MRD....

There was a big capital gain on the old stock and even a loss on some of the IRA stock (which could be used to offset some active income for the grandchild .)

The moral of the story is that life (and Federal tax) is so complex that the average citizen today doesn't have a chance of doing it right. But now, 55 years after I took Taxation in law school, I am smart enough to know which stock to give grandkids in the future. If we keep doing it, it will be MRD stock from the IRA— and no more stock from the RVW ("old") account....

4/25/07

Chapter 47

REQUIEM FOR A LIBERTARIAN

A FAVORITE MANTRA OF the lingering libertarian mindset in America is that "The least governed people is the best governed people." That may have had plausibility when Jefferson pronounced it 200 years ago, but it is dangerously fatuous in the year 2000. The Freemen, Militia types, and other redneck advocates of government rejection are latter-day retarded adolescents who confuse anarchy and self-indulgence with freedom and security.

The reason the current anti-government sentiment is juvenile and anachronistic is two-fold. First, the need for group consensus and discipline is directly proportionate to the density of population. In short, the closer the neighbors, the greater the probability of friction between neighbors ... the raw material of conflict and physical battle. I call it the Wills Propinquity Principle—the closer the ranks, the greater the risk of conflict. And the greater the need for an enforced code of conduct, which is the essence of government.

THE POPULATION EXPLOSION WILL bring humans closer and closer together. And the communication explosion will demonstrate more graphically the disparity between the Haves and the Have-nots, which is the powder keg for civil commotion and insurrection, which remain the evils that group discipline (ultimately called government), was calculated to avoid.

The second trend militating against individual self-determination is a perceived erosion of self-discipline and personal responsibility. Whether you elect to blame the decline of the basic family unit, accelerating pressures on middleclass youth to succeed, unfortunate demographic trends, or the decline in the influence of organized religion, the social result is the same. Individuals need more external control, not less. Corruption, fraud, predatory practices, and bunko are rife in both government and business. Citizens demand more protection from crime and predation, and more compensation for torts and misadventures—yet they resent the very governments that provide the police, the armed services, and the courts.

When it comes right down to it, the average American wants more and more services and protection from government—and will do so in the future—but he seems to resent government more and more, wants it reduced, and wants to pay less for it.

The result of this schizophrenia, partially promulgated by the Republican party, will be either more and more government in the 21st century or periods of civil commotion, disaffection, and riot, which will in the end produce martial law, the most arbitrary and forceful form of government. The less noble the American citizen becomes, the more he will have to be managed. And the more frustrated and irritable he becomes, the more he will have to be intimidated.

The age of Rousseau and Thoreau is past. Self determination has become, or is destined to be, a rhetorical concept.

6/21/00
Second the motion, 8/11/11

Chapter 48

Scanning the Horizon for Net Worth Or Reading Your Way to Wealth

It's one thing to watch an event or a trend in action, and still another to view it in retrospect. But the real trick is to see it coming—and prepare for it, or do something about it. Foresight is the ticket—to equanimity, if not success.

If you see far enough around the curve—ahead of the crowd—and do something about it, the result can be protective, as well as satisfying. And if what you see on the horizon has economic aspects, it can be profitable to beat the crowd's reaction.

I'm not talking about crystal ball gazing or premonition. No "little bird" has ever told me anything. And I'm not interested in garden variety pundits. I'm talking about the perception that comes from keen observation of current events and current trends—by the naked eye, the naked newspaper, the naked periodical. I'm talking about extending cause and effect beyond the current scene to the next logical or historical step, whether crisis or bonanza. It's not rocket science in terms of complexity. But it does require a special talent in terms of acute observation and an extensive harvest of information, through reading (obviously nonfiction), travel, television, and life experience (i.e., age.)

Some of my foresights have been profitable because I acted on them slightly ahead of the crowd. They were obvious trends based on unavoidable statistics. For example, the graying of America was obvious two or three decades ago, based on population and life expectancy growth, But how many saw it soon enough to invest in Big Pharma stocks while they were still cheap? Then how many saw the bonanza start to fade in the last decade because of political attacks on Big Pharma profits, the fading drug pipelines and patents, the push of government and HMOs to generics instead of patented drugs, and the chilling effect of class action litigation?

Because of those forces in the late 20th Century, a decade ago I made a switch from Big Pharma to medical equipment, devices, and supplies, all relatively free of political and litigation assaults, yet riding the surge of an aging population and the public appetite for more health care.

The other unavoidable crisis that loomed on the horizon ten or fifteen years ago—and again doubled our net worth—was the oil and gas crunch of recent years. It was coming for over a decade: the U.S. hasn't built a refinery for 35 years (!) and oil slid to prices that

Robert V. Wills

discouraged exploration and production in the U.S.

Meanwhile, U.S. vehicles got bigger and hungrier, while at the same time China and India—40% of the earth's population—discovered the internal combustion engine and clean-burning natural gas. What happened was as inevitable as Spring rain. Fortunately, I bought most of my energy stocks while sweet crude was still $50-$60 a barrel and natural gas was half the current btu price.

Incidentally, I'm not ready to abandon energy stocks yet, because alternative energy sources are still a lovely dream, oil and gas companies make juicy profits even at $100 a barrel, and the inevitable nuclear plants will take five to nine years to build and get on line.

Another coming crisis that has investment potential is the parching of America, particularly the semi-arid tropical regions of the Southwest. Thanks to unbridled development in California, Arizona, and Nevada, with no development of additional water sources like desalinization, or diversion from the Northwest (isn't unregulated capitalism grand?) the Southwest will inevitably face severe drought in the next decade.

Even banning the ridiculous aerial irrigation in the San Joaquin and Imperial Valleys won't solve the problem. Furthermore, a secondary effect of the parching of Western America will be the continuing rash of wildfires, which themselves exacerbate the water shortage problem by diverting huge quantities of water to fire fighting.

Radical changes in the use and price of water are coming, so invest accordingly. Water resources ETF would be a good starting point.

ANOTHER SAD DEVELOPMENT IS the U.S. economic eclipse of the last three years, another product of unregulated capitalism in action. It is really a mini-depression, not a recession. Tens of millions are affected—foreclosures, layoffs, bankruptcies—so disposable income is tight, even for the middle class, and discretionary income is even tighter. So is it any wonder that the "big box" superstores (WalMart, Costco) are on the rise, not to mention the discount outlets (Big Lots, 99 Cents Only stores, Thrift stores). I see a continued rise in these stocks. And don't overlook cheap entertainment in hard times, like pizza parlors and DVD rentals.

Two observations that helped to feed, or at least shield, our net worth were an aversion to legal partnerships and an aversion to paying off landlords' mortgages. Over a span of 20 years, I employed nine attorneys and paid them well—and put their names in lights—but avoided the pitfalls of legal partnership. I had seen too many legal partnerships break up bitterly to run the risk. Something about lawyers, I'm afraid.

After three years of paying office rent to a very nice guy, I bought an old house facing a nice Tustin park, scraped it, got an architect with a little flair, and had a master carpenter friend build a two-story-over-garage office building with an atrium and a little panache. I probably sold it too soon, in 2000, to a friend. Now I miss it, but not the maintenance problems and expense. And my resulting medical equipment and device stocks have probably gone up in market value more than the building.

Some would say that we've been very lucky to have prospered in the law firm, real estate, and stock markets, especially dealing mostly in equities and not bonds or mutual funds. But I don't think so. The decision to build early, home, then office, and to buy equity in promising markets, rather than bonds and mutual funds for yield, were not luck. They were the result of watching the horizon, reading a lot, and taking some chances. With risk there can be reward. And with an eye on the horizon, you may be able to stay a step or two ahead of the crowd.

9/2/08

Chapter 49

ON CONTEMPLATING THORNS
AND SEED BALLS

WOULD THERE BE ROSES without thorns? Would there be liquidambar trees without seed balls? Probably not in this world, where everything beautiful or exceptional comes at a cost or with risk. The roses are protected by thorns that puncture and lacerate the careless. The multicolored liquidambars are perpetuated by countless spiked seed balls that litter the ground for months after their palette of leaves is gone.

How many other of life's pleasures carry a latent cost or risk? So many that we have come to sense that "if your cup runneth over, looketh out." ... Every hot streak runs out. Even life itself, sweet as it may become, has its sting, the ultimate endpoint—death. That's a risk we can't dodge, or even insure against.

But we can still smell the roses and feast on the Fall colors, and live a full and exciting life—despite the risks and the penalties.

3/12/08

Chapter 50

HAVE YOU NOTICED ABOUT REPUBLICANS?

A Republican is a person who is death on tax increases, but who always increases government spending and the Federal deficit and the national debt—as did Reagan, Bush, and Bush, all in dramatic fashion.

A Republican is a person who rails against welfare and social programs as liberal giveaways, but who abolishes family planning and contraception programs—and who campaigns against abortion as did Reagan, Bush, and Bush.

A Republican is a proud advocate of laissez faire economics and the free market, and rails against government regulation at all levels, but who produces economic scandals like the S&L crisis, the Resolution Trust crisis, the Enron scandal, and the current mortgage banking disaster, as did Reagan, Bush, and Bush.

A Republican is a super patriot flag waver who

stands for America First, My Country Right or Wrong, and who regards foreigners as either slightly inferior, quaint, or a threat to our security, and who therefore supports a large military budget über alles, as did Reagan, Bush, and Bush.

A Republican is a person who extols individual freedom and denigrates government per se as the ultimate problem, but who champions Law and Order, harsher sentences, deportation of illegals, and strong immigration barriers.

A Republican is a formidable political opponent who is a firm believer in dirty tricks, a la Richard Nixon's burglary and enemies list, George Bush Senior's Willy Horton ads, George Bush Junior's Swift Boat campaign and other Karl Rove tricks, and McCain's stealth campaign to paint Obama as Muslim and a Weatherman radical. Democrats are feeble street fighters and are easily confounded by Republican dirty tricks....

A Republican tends to be a God-fearing, churchgoing Populist who wants God in the legislature and the classroom, as well as on our coins and public buildings, all in spite of the First Amendment and Thomas Jefferson's advice. (However, not all Republicans follow the talk radio theme on that one, and I certainly didn't.).

A Republican stoutly believes that he is on the side of the common man, constantly referring to Main Street, but actually favors Wall Street in his voting on tax and business issues, declaring that "what's good for General Motors is good for America." Corporations and those of us earning more than $250,000 relish the tax programs of Reagan, Bush, and Bush.

The most modern brand of Republican, the neo-con, believes that America should use its dominant military and economic position to crush hostile political regimes, either by invasion (if small and weak enough, like Vietnam and Grenada, and Iraq), or by embargo (Cuba), or by huffing and puffing (North Korea, Iran).

The Neocon is a dedicated supporter of Israel because it adheres to our political philosophy and it is surrounded and menaced by Islamic states that he dislikes and distrusts.

A Republican traditionally preaches monetary conservatism and fiscal responsibility, all the while running up historic deficits, a la Reagan, Bush, and Bush, and spawning an ungodly swarm of lobbyists and influence peddlers, a la Abramoff, and a covey of crooked legislators, a la Ted Stevens, Tom Delay, Spiro Agnew, and Sam Cunningham. Under Reagan, Bush, and Bush, the national debt soared like never before, but I don't know any other voter but me who keeps charts on the budget, the deficit, and the national debt.

So the Republicans are rarely called to account for their fiscal irresponsibility because the average American voter is lost in the woods.

After about 40 years of scoffing at the Democrats, these are a few of the reasons I stopped being a Republican during Reagan's second term.

9/26/08

Chapter 51

The Libertarian
Trickle Down Fallacy

EVEN THE ARCHITECTS OF the U.S. Constitution realized, 230 years ago, that, left unchecked by governmental oversight and regulation, men's basic ambitions and impulses would lead to conflict, corruption, and chaos. The Articles of Confederation provided no control or discipline and proved the point dramatically.

What Americans can't grasp at this late date is that the basic premise and philosophy of the Republican and Libertarian parties is based on the same fallacy that produced the Articles of Confederation—the notion that left unchecked man's initiative and energy will produce the optimum prosperity, and that wealth will trickle down from the most successful to the least.

Nothing could be further from the truth. The economic policies of Reagan, Bush, and Bush—with a staggering national debt and a perilous widening gap between the haves and the have-nots—are exhibit A for the fallacy. Maybe on November 4 a majority of American voters will *finally* turn away two more disciples of the wearisome and flawed Republican anti-government mantra.

10/20/08

Chapter 52

ON SUPREME COURT DECISIONS

A WORD OR TWO ABOUT constitutional law, my favorite subject in law school. Supreme Court Justice Clarence Thomas recently gave interviews while promoting his autobiography and, in discussing the abortion issue, he made what I regard as an asinine statement for a lawyer, much less a judge. He says he merely follows the language of the Constitution, no doubt regarding himself as a "strict constructionist." Any true constitutional lawyer knows that the framers of the Constitution in 1789 had no notion of the complexities of modern society two-and-a-quarter centuries later, and merely set forth a government plan based on eighteenth century ideals and experience, basically a manual—a set of bylaws—for the mechanics of a new democracy.

It was not until the first 10 amendments ("The Bill of Rights") were drafted and adopted in 1791 that specific individual rights were defined, in the broadest of terms, again based on 18th century bad experience with the tyrannies of Kings and Popes and Czars and Archbishops. How could they possibly lay out rules that would answer 21st century questions about abortion, school segregation, gangs, handguns, zoning, reapportionment, and eminent domain?

They couldn't, and they didn't.

All a 2007 Supreme Court Justice can do is try to divine the intentions of the framers by interpolation and inference from what they did write, and from a survey of the societal context in which the Constitution was drafted. This obviously leaves acres of room for different conclusions, as the endless 5-4 decisions demonstrate. Any court realist knows that the broad generic language of the Constitution—as they say, so broad you can drive a truck through it—allows the personal philosophical and political temperament of the judge to play a role in his decision.

When you recognize that every Supreme Court appointment is a political appointment by a president anxious to advance his own political and social ideology, you recognize the utter hypocrisy of Thomas claiming that he will just be interpreting the language of the framers in voting to overturn Roe v. Wade or upholding the provision of the so-called Patriot Act.

No issue so simple that it is covered unequivocally by Constitutional language would ever make it up three levels to the U.S. Supreme Court. For example, it's only because the Second Amendment language is somewhat equivocal that the Court will be deciding whether D.C. can ban handguns in the hands of private citizens. And it's only because the framers never dealt with abortion in any manner that a politically appointed Court can do anything they want with it—ban late term abortions, affirm Roe v. Wade, or overrule it. Due process won't solve the problem because "due process" is essentially a political concept and has no immutable definition.

12/1/07

Chapter 53

On Tattoos

I DON'T CARE HOW popular tattoos become, or how many middle-class teens get them. They are a visible brand of utter stupidity. Whether it is tattoos or eyebrow rings or tongue studs or lip saucers, people who deface or deform their bodies are fools at best and morons at worst.

It's one thing for a drunken sailor to get tattooed in some seamy dive in a grungy port. It's another for teenage girls and college athletes to vandalize their bodies with permanent graffiti or primitive disfigurement.

Let the dermatologists and plastic surgeons double their fees as a penalty for self-mutilation when they try to undo the damage.

7/15/01
Second the motion, 8/11/11

Chapter 54

WHAT CAN TURN THE
GOLDEN YEARS TO LEAD

SOME OF THE SHINE comes off when you realize that:

- Your parents are dead and gone, and with them your only source of early family history;

- Your long-time friends are dead or dying or in eldercare facilities;

- Your family patronizes you and makes allowances for you as an elder;

- Your hearing loss causes you to miss a lot of casual or group conversation;

- You can't read anything without magnification;

- Your body is stiff and achy until your NSAID takes hold;

- You don't feel good until your coffee kicks in;

- You can no longer tolerate, much less take pleasure in, confusion;

- You are appalled at how much kids don't know, and wonder how they will ever survive;

- You think the whole culture has gone cheap and coarse (which, of course, it has ...);

- You are repulsed by the endless moronic advertising on network TV;

- The American public looks mongrel-ized and Third World;

- Your feet get both numb and hypersensitive;

- You get sleepy after dinner, but have trouble getting to sleep later;

- You make less and less progress on your project list;

- You lose all faith in the American electorate (for good reason), and expect the worst:

- You observe a diminishing literacy and vocabulary on all sides;

- You vow to resume an exercise regime but remain too stiff to get started...then your energy runs out;

- Your list of desired dinner companions shrinks as more people seem too talkative;

- You are as observant of feminine charms as ever, but perfectly happy to remain an appreciative and perceptive observer;

157

- You give away more show biz and concert tickets because the outings take energy and more and more you enjoy a quiet evening at home.

- You are no longer interested in an automobile trip with more than a hundred miles of road time;

- You don't travel far by air in economy class;

- You would never again get under a car or up on the roof, and will avoid all caves and caverns;

- You can't take high altitude without tachycardia;

- You minimize time in bright sun, and won't swim in water that's not a coral sea;

- You can't imagine how educated adults can be that conservative or that religious, and deliberately minimize time spent with either group;

- You find most social conversation inane or vacuous;

- You find that most people in your age group have two main topics of information—their amazing grandchildren (a Can You Top This? Contest) and their latest ailments and doctors' visits (an "organ recital");

- You have trouble deciding what to throw away;

BUT
- You realize that you've outlived half of your high school classmates already, you are healthier than 80% of your age group, you're smarter than 90% of your contemporaries, and
- You can write stuff like this....

8/10/06

Chapter 55

On Justice in General and Jury Verdicts in Particular: A Trial Lawyer's Retrospective

W HEN I STARTED TRIAL work in downtown L.A. fifty-one years ago, the courthouse was called The Hall of Justice. It was a noble concept, but we have come a very long way since 1954 and no one would ever think of a courthouse today as a "hall of justice." Certainly not an experienced trial lawyer who has won cases he knew he should lose and lost cases he should have won.

A much more accurate title for a courthouse today would be The Hall of Adjudication or The Hall of Mediation. We are now sophisticated enough to know that "justice" is a concept and an ideal, a moral sense, perhaps only a personal intuition.

Present any group a given set of facts and ask them to define a "just" outcome and you will quickly discover how personal and how subjective the concept of justice is. Any trial lawyer knows the unpredictable nature of a jury—they have seen the same evidence for days or weeks, yet reach different conclusions. When the jurors bring such different backgrounds, experience, and biases to the jury room, I don't know how prosecutors ever convince twelve people to agree on anything "beyond a reasonable doubt"—even that the sun will come up tomorrow. We rarely got a 12-0 verdict in civil cases, which require only agreement on what the "preponderance of the evidence" showed. It's in recognition of the diversity of human attitudes and reactions that in California we require only 9 votes out of 12 for a civil verdict.

Because of the unpredictability of juries, the inordinate time and expense involved in a jury trial, and the logjam of civil cases in our courts, the "growth industry" in the legal profession is called ADR—alternative dispute resolution—also referred to as mediation or arbitration.

Several decades ago the California courts adopted a procedure whereby civil cases having what a supervising judge felt was limited monetary value, were assigned to mandatory arbitration before a judge or attorney volunteer. The decision of the arbitrator was not final if one party moved to return the case to the trial calendar, but there are disincentives to do so and most cases do not return—or they settle. The arbitration procedure is actually a second effort to dispose of a civil case because the case may already have been set for a mandatory settlement conference in the courthouse, either before or after it goes off to arbitration.

More and more retired attorneys and judges, plus a growing number of attorneys still in practice, have set themselves up as arbitrators or mediators. Today, fewer and fewer civil cases go to a jury. The courts have budgetary problems and an ever-increasing criminal caseload. Criminal cases have priority over civil, so a large proportion of the court budgets goes to the processing and trial of the criminal cases, which is further reason for the growth of the ADR "business."

Settlement is also the watchword on the criminal side of the court system. Compromise dispositions there are called plea bargains instead of settlements, but the goal is the same—to reduce the load on the courts and avoid the unpredictability of juries.

I should also add that "the vicissitudes of trial" refer not only to jury risk, but also the idiosyncrasies of judges, all of whom are individuals with varied experience, attitudes, biases, and emotional temperament— and all of whom were political appointees....

The same elusive quality of "justice" is demonstrated daily in the Halls of Congress, the White House, and the state capitols. If a politician turned theoretical, he would probably define his job as the pursuit of security and order, not "justice." Like the average citizen, he would regard "justice" as the goal of the courts, not the legislature or the executive mansion. The politician sees himself as basically engaged in the management of money and the preservation of order. He would say—or should say—that he leaves the job of balancing the "scales of justice" to the courts; picture the fair maiden who is blindfolded, yet holding out a scale and presumably trying to balance it. Or, in the age of pragmatism, does anyone even see that image anymore?

When you stop to think about it, even the courts are also basically involved in the preservation of order and the management of money. Isn't a lawsuit a refined substitute for an alley fight or a plunder by force, both of which would upset the social order ... and isn't a criminal case an attempt to preserve social order by avoiding revenge and violence?

So when we talk about justice we are really referring to an attempt to satisfy individual notions of fairness. And since individual notions of fairness roam all over the map, who would be surprised to discover that justice is more a shining ideal than an achievable goal? In the end, justice is our own personal concept of a just or fair resolution of a problem, not a definable, attainable end result.

Remember that the next time you are faced with a jury of your "peers" (?!) or are trying to comprehend what a judge or jury has delivered....

6/8/05

Chapter 56

THE STARS WERE LINED UP RIGHT

L IKE SO MANY TURNS IN LIFE, my becoming a lawyer was pretty much a happy accident. We had no lawyers in the family and no one before I was 22 years old had ever suggested that I should consider law school. At the University of Hawaii and San Jose State College, my academic interest had gravitated to the biological and social sciences, but two courses in chemistry at Stanford in 1948 put a damper on medicine, which had never been a serious goal for me anyhow.

As a result of engineering courses at Stanford and Oregon State College while a 17 year old in the ASTRP (Army Specialized Training Reserve Program), then biology courses at the University of Hawaii and later San Jose State, I had a Bachelor's degree that was as generic and non-specific as my academic career had been—a B.A. in Biological and Physical Sciences.

I was loosely headed for a masters or doctorate degree in psychology at UCLA when several con-current events changed the course of my life. We will never know whether I would have made a mark as a psychometrist, but I had taken and passed the graduate reading exam at UCLA and was interested in combining psychology and/or physiology with statistics to break some new ground in the field of human behavior.

The first step in my redirection came in the form of a pronouncement by Maralys while I was lying under our old car in the driveway of our little house in Encino. I can't recall what I was working on, maybe just changing the oil, but Maralys had just read my latest letter to the builders of our new little house, reciting our latest litany of complaints about what had been a three month comedy of errors by a pair of novice builders. I had apparently muffled our exasperation so well that Maralys admired both my restraint and my prose. Her comment was to the effect that "you ought to be a lawyer" because I had sounded so much like one in my dealings with the two young greenhorn builders.

The timing of the opinion was fortuitous because UCLA had recently announced its plans to open a law school in Westwood that would be the "Harvard Law School of the West" or something as impressive. The timing was also right for me to take the Law School Admissions Test (LSAT), if I were so inclined, and shortly I was. To make a long story short, I not only took the LSAT, but received a score in the 99th percentile, which not only corroborated M's opinion in spades but facilitated admission to UCLA Law School's class of 1953.

The rest, as they say, is history. I didn't set the world on fire in my three years of law school, but I did get off to a good start, ranking #2 in the middle of our first year and 12th at the end. More about the moot court adventure later.

I'm not sure that law was the only right course for my constitution, but I think most who have known me since 1953 would think so. Although law school was an ordeal of sorts, it offered a broad vista of life and led to three different careers, one corporate and two in litigation.

I recall concluding during and after law school that I felt it was an intellectual exercise that I would recommend to any of my children, whether they intended to practice law or not. It is certainly not an exercise that many could afford, especially today, but I am happy that one son and one granddaughter have experienced it and know what I meant.

2/4/05

Chapter 57

Ephemera:
The Loss of Life's Landmarks

THE BANE OF ADVANCED AGE is physical and organic breakdown. But the demoralization of long life I blame on the growing awareness of ephemera, the disappearance of human and physical landmarks that became part of us.

It isn't just Ipana tooth paste and Rinso and Lincoln Logs and Lionel trains. It's the Studebaker and Packard—and now Oldsmobile. It's Pan Am, TWA, Eastern, National, Western, and Air Cal, and Hughes Air West. It's Tom Mix and Charles Chaplin, Merle Oberon, Carole Lombard, and Mae West, Lawrence Olivier and Burt Lancaster. It's our grandparents, then both parents....

It's the popular songs of the Forties and Fifties, *The Ed Sullivan* show, *The Honeymooners*, and *St. Elsewhere*. And now *The Johnnie Carson Show*.

It's sitcoms without raunch. It's the slang of our youth; our grandkids know none of it (nor do we appreciate theirs). It's most childhood friends. In my case, it's even the family home in my high school years. Not only is the house gone. So is the street. As though it never existed, except in a dream....

Every funeral reminds us how transitory our personal contacts are. And every old Christmas card list has the names of lost or forgotten friends. Are they dead? Why did we drift apart so completely? Will the list change entirely if we live long enough? (And don't try to locate friends of 25 or 30 years ago; the men have moved, probably twice, and the women have also moved or have new names ...)

The question becomes, if we live long enough, will we be adrift in a remote, alien world, surrounded by people who talk differently, know nothing about what happened more then 25 years ago, and regard us as relics of a dead age?

Not a pretty thought. But as I watch network TV and listen to grandkids—or even young professionals—talk, and read the newspapers and popular magazines, I feel more and more estranged and disconnected, if not repulsed. I wonder if I am consigned to the company of people my own age, if we are to have anything in common, not a happy prospect because of the prevalence of eccentricity and narrow perspective ... Are we to be relegated to the company of cranks, dyspeptics, die hards, curmudgeons, and crones—not to mention bored or impatient caretakers who are underpaid and underskilled?

No, thank you. I hope to be able to avoid the exclusive company of both the very young—who seem to know almost nothing—and also the truly geriatric, whose minds were set in concrete years ago and whose two interests in life may be grandchildren and bodily functions. With sufficient resources we can survey the arts in show biz, study strangers on trips to sparkling retreats, and be selective in our relationships with seniors. And—the hardest part of all—we can keep our mind slightly ajar even though we think we know it all and the "golden years" are long, long gone....

1/30/05

Chapter 58

A Deadly Cocktail: Procreation and Fundamentalist Theology

In the Western world, copulation is a celebrated and commercially promoted indoor sport requiring no athletic talent or net worth. In the absence of birth control efforts, it results in repeated pregnancies. Fortunately, therapeutic abortion is still legal in most countries, and a lot cheaper than childbirth.

However, in the U.S., a combination of fundamentalist Christians and Republican politicians is campaigning hard to force pregnant women to deliver their babies, regardless of whether they want, or can afford to raise, the children. And, to add insult to injury, these same ideological tyrants, through congressional action, have effectively blocked family counseling and birth control availability in both the free world and the third world.

In the Eastern world, particularly sub-Saharan Africa, the Muslim countries, and Southern Asia, copulation is a cost-free escape from grinding poverty and deprivation—basically the only recreation that young males enjoy—and the women are powerless to prevent pregnancy, even if they already have starving children. Instead of sending food to those pathetic multitudes, we should be sending birth control supplies and agricultural instructors.

As a result of high birth rates in such countries as Nigeria, Uganda, Algeria, Iraq, and Bangladesh, the earth's population, now 6.3 billion, is expected to reach nine billion by 2050, despite low birth rates in the U.S., the U.K., China, and Japan ... a 50% increase in the planet's population in just 50 years.

The only events that could alter the population explosion are all grim—with the exception of a complete overhaul of the U.S. government, a squelching of the theological forces, a worldwide empowerment of women, and a world summit on birth control programs. The ideology of the U.S. at this time is 180 degrees in the wrong direction.

The un-pretty events that could defuse the population bomb are famine, plague, massive civil unrest, and nuclear holocaust. They are all depressing to contemplate, but some may occur, particularly since the gap between the haves and the have-nots in the world is widening, and the risk of civil unrest magnifies as the middle class disappears.

The have-nots portion of the population is increasing, while the affluent limit birth rates, so the risk of revolution will grow as water and food shortages become acute. For awhile, only mass desalinization of water and major advances in agriculture can stem the tide. But the only benign and long-term defense against the population bomb must be universal birth control … with family counseling, sex education, and therapeutic abortions available without stigma or obstruction.

Water pollution will exacerbate the water supply problem, and atmospheric pollution will compete with it for first place as a health hazard when the earth's population is not only 50% larger, but the third world moves from bicycles and oxcarts and family farms to internal combustion engines and factories. China and India alone make up 37.4% of the earth's population and are rapidly becoming industrialized and motorized, increasing air and water pollution—plus competition for the world's shrinking oil supplies.

You may not have noticed that a pharmaceutical company (Barr) long ago developed a morning-after contraceptive known as Plan B. Last year an FDA committee of scientists tested and approved it for non-prescription sale. The FDA rarely goes against its advisory committees, but the Bush White House intervened and quashed the pill pending "further study," obviously on theological grounds. The FDA is scheduled to act on the matter again in September.

Thus a combination of ideology and theology threatens Armageddon in this century. Fifty years ago, I worried about the A-Bomb and the H-bomb darkening our children's future. I still do: you can't unleash weapons like that on civilian populations without having it turn on you in time … and America's dedicated enemies are already planning nuclear retribution on us—made likelier by a Republican congress that has refused to pay Russia to round up all of its loosely-secured cold war nuclear material.

So the future looks very dicey, even before the population bomb explodes in 10 or 20 years. We are leaving our children a life or death set of problems. I just wish we could hand them the world we inherited in the first half of the 20th century.

7/21/05

Chapter 59

Epiphany:
A Lesson of Epic Proportions

I N MY THIRD YEAR of law school I became a member of a two-man team assigned to represent UCLA Law School in a moot court competition between the major law schools of California. There were then four law schools in Southern California and three in the North. We were assigned one side of a constitutional law case on appeal and scheduled to brief the case, then face one of the other schools in oral argument.

The case involved a California well-spacing statute that limited the number of oil wells in a given area for the purpose of preventing unsightly clustering of oil well structures above ground and unfair tapping into the oil structure below ground.* The legislation was probably a reaction to the pincushion development of some oil fields in the early 20th century.

We were assigned the appellate side of the case, meaning that we were attacking the statute as unconstitutional, and the opposing school was defending it as reasonable regulation, and thereby constitutional. Our first opponent was Loyola Law School, a worthy rival. Daren Johnson and I were selected to present the oral argument before a panel of real judges in very formal fashion. I had to buy a dark suit for the occasion (and didn't have much to spend in those days, so cut corners somehow).

By the time we argued the case, we were thoroughly convinced of the righteousness of our position. Our opponents were impressive, presumably the best that Loyola could throw at us. But we won the first round, then had to face the winner from the other Southern California round—USC, our archrival.

I don't know whether the other winning team represented the appellant, too, but if they did, they lost a coin toss because in the second round Daren and I were still representing the appellant. We couldn't imagine otherwise because we knew we were right .

We were at or near the end of our third year, and graduation, when we won the second round—and would face the winning team from the Northern schools at the State Bar Convention to be held in Monterey in September.

Fortunately, that was a few days after the Bar exam, which would keep us more than occupied for the summer. After three years of law school, passing the Bar exam was critical, and passing was anything but certain, even after graduating from a top law school. And, to add to the confusion, Maralys was pregnant with Eric and scheduled to deliver within a week or two of the Bar Convention, and our *big event* there.

We got through graduation, a couple of months of the Bar Review course, then the three day Bar exam in a hot, humid, non-airconditioned Embassy Auditorium in downtown Los Angeles. Next came the drive to Monterey in our old Nash car.

But the biggest stress came from the fact that we had lost the coin toss and had to switch our brief and our argument to the Respondent—the other side that we had soundly beaten twice, and with real conviction. What kind of chance would we have arguing the wrong side of the case???

Somehow we turned out a new brief and headed to Monterey to take our lumps. I was already working in the Legal Department of Liberty Mutual in downtown L.A., so was tired from the commuting and the Bar exam preparation.

We started for Monterey late enough so it was already dark. Unfortunately, the old Nash had no reading light and the dome light operated only with the door open, so in order to read my case papers (as M. drove) I had to keep the passenger door ajar with an empty milk bottle.

The trip was tough enough without our additional handicap—newborn Eric in the backseat. My parents no doubt had Bobby and Chris, but M. was breastfeeding, as always, and Eric was only days old, so along he came to Monterey.

We had no chance for a good night's sleep because we got into a Monterey hotel quite late and were due at the Convention early the next morning. Air hammers outside at five a.m. ruined what few hours we had in bed. So in the morning I was a tired and semi-frantic 26-year-old, too nauseated to eat the breakfast M. had ordered.

The argument was held in a large meeting or convention hall, with some imposing, real appellate judges sitting en banc on the stage. The audience consisted of members of the California Bar attending the convention and not otherwise occupied at that early hour. Maralys had stashed Eric somewhere for my argument and was worried about my fatigue and tension.

But the fatigue turned out to be a blessing in disguise, because by the time I addressed the Court I appeared cool, calm, and composed. I was too tired to be tense, so my dreamlike state and measured pace must have conveyed both confidence and poise. And, amazing enough, by then I had come to believe in the Respondent's case....

The attorneys who drafted the case for us to labor over must have been very bright indeed, because the case obviously had two arguable sides, which is not always the situation. But having turned our minds 180 degrees and completely realigned our convictions taught me a lesson I should never forget. I guess the lesson is that you should never set your mind in concrete because, under most circumstances, you can never be 100% right. It's OK, often essential, to take a firm position. But don't be surprised if others see things differently. They may be looking at the facts from a different angle, or applying different criteria or values.

Daren Johnson, being a motormouth and an experienced debater, was no doubt shocked when, among the four advocates, the judges awarded me the prize for Best Oral Argument. I carried home Wests California Digest and numerous other law volumes. Needless to say, in my stuperous-but-elated state, I enjoyed the congratulations from attending attorneys. I wouldn't have been prouder wearing the Congressional Medal of Honor.

2/10/05

*Roger Blackgold vs. UR Dutybound

Chapter 60

CATHY'S LEGACY

As a teenager I had a love affair that significantly altered my long life. It altered my emotional makeup, my taste in women, my travels for 40 years, and my personal identification with, and friendships in, the United Kingdom. I have never fully recovered.

The spell was set in the Yorkshire Moors, to which I have returned many times and will always return. My tryst with Cathy Earnshaw, a headstrong Yorkshire beauty, commenced in a black-and-white fantasy set in the crags of the moors of the West Riding. Years later I transposed the setting in my psyche to Skelton's tower, near Levisham, in the North Riding.

There the moors reach out for miles across Newton Dale, and the only signs of civilization are a distant microwave "golf ball" on a high ridge and an abandoned railway track in the glen, stretching from Pickering to Whitby on the North Sea. Only sheep populate the expanse of heather on the slopes. A grove of evergreens stands across the glen below. The only sounds are the wind and occasionally the bleat of a distant sheep.

Reverend Skelton abandoned his isolated retreat decades ago, leaving the stone tower to the ravages of occasional village youths who could not resist sending pieces of it down the glen slopes. Nevertheless what's left of it stands as a lonely sentinel on the brow of the glen, strangely silent about its history.

Whereas Reverend Skelton no doubt scanned the endless sky for ecclesiastical inspiration—he reportedly composed his sermons there—I surveyed the heather moors in the hopes that Cathy Earnshaw might again appear, dark tresses flowing and dark eyes firing my youthful passion. How could she be so frivolous and capricious in an idyll like this, with an ardent male intoxicated by the cocktail of her feminine allure and the isolation of our heather bower? Were not we and this idyll the ultimate Eden, so nothing else in the world mattered?

Cathy Earnshaw never appeared … But I never forgot the crags, the heather, and what almost was. It was no coincidence that I returned to my substitute Eden many times in 40 years, and will probably do so while I can still ambulate the mile or so across the moor from the village of Levisham.

The journey from the crags in the West Riding to Skelton's Tower in the North Riding was like many twists in life, a series of happy accidents. It all started in downtown Honolulu when I was a student at the University of Hawaii after WW II, and saw the 1939 movie, *Wuthering Heights*, with Laurence Olivier as Heathcliffe and Merle Oberon as Cathy Earnshaw. I never forgot her.

The next step in my quest took place in 1962 at my desk in a corporate suite in Long Beach, when Maralys and I were scheduled to fly SAS to Europe with a Los Angeles Bar Association group. I knew that we would get to England and the moors, so I studied a map of Yorkshire and picked a town called Malton, east of York, as a starting point for a trek onto the moors in search of Cathy. A great deal of personal history grew out of that selection so long ago.

Using our Britrail pass, we arrived in York by train, then rode a smoke-filled bus to Malton, a graphic illustration of how much the British smoked forty years ago. We had no reservations, which was routine for us in our adventuresome youth.

The Village of Malton was manageable on foot and we soon found ourselves admitted at a large converted girls' school, now a hotel called The Mount, no doubt because it did sit atop a mount of sorts.

The heart of The Mount was the pub, and we soon met two brothers in their forties, Wilf and Jim Wise, who were not only gregarious but obviously regular patrons of the pub. We were fascinated by the whole setting—the yellow cast in the night air outside from

Malton's mercury street lamps, the cheery glow in the pub, and the welcome congeniality of Wilf Wise (Jim was older and more tentative). It was on that October night in 1962 that we forged a lifelong friendship with a legendary storyteller and one of the most sanguine, generous, and competent individuals we have ever met.

It turned out that Wilf Wise—we mistakenly called him "Wolf" for the first 30 years—was a solicitor who became an RAF bomber pilot during the early war years, was shot down over Germany, and was the only survivor of his crew, thanks to holding his breath during several minutes of fire. He was the highest ranking officer in the German POW camp, somehow escaped, but was recaptured because of the cowardice of a fellow escapee, and rode out the war as a POW. He never returned to the practice of law. Instead he became a very successful "corn broker" in Yorkshire, meaning that he was the middleman between the farmers and the breweries. "Corn" was not "corn" as we know it, but actually barley and malt, primary commodities to be sure in Yorkshire.

To make a long story short, in the early days we played tennis on clay with Wilf and Jim, were later given the use of a company Morris Oxford for a tour of Scotland, Ireland, and the Midlands, and have stayed in the four-story Wise home ("Daleside") overlooking Scarborough Harbor on almost every trip during the last 30 years.

Wilf drove us all over the moors, from Pickering to Goathland to Whitby, and all points in between. He introduced us to the Levisham Pub, then Skelton's Tower, Pickering Castle, the stepping stones at Egton, Thornton-Le-Dale, and Robins Hood Bay.

He showed us the pheasant farm he tended for his hunting chums. He read stories to the blind. While at a fishing "chalet" in Northumberland, he took us to a castle where they were filming a James Bond movie. And recently, since Wilf died in his 80s, his oldest son, an actor in London, took us to Oliver's Mount and Scarborough Castle.

Although Wilf was forever jovial and a master storyteller, since WW II he rose above additional tragedy. His first wife died of cancer many years ago. A second son from the first marriage was institutionalized with CP. He lost the sight of an eye in a hunting accident. But Wilf was fortunate to marry Helen, a beautiful younger woman, and to raise a second family of bright daughters. Helen still manages Daleside and has thus far resisted our efforts to have her visit us here (as two other British couples did 25 years ago).

Wilf and Jim Wise are now gone, so our visits to Skelton's Tower will be more difficult. We prefer British trains to British driving. But there is no need to trek to Levisham to see Cathy again. I need only put in the tape of Wuthering Heights to see Merle Oberon recreate that spell in the crags on the Yorkshire Moors

… I can cry again when she dies, as I always have.

All's well that ends well. I married a far more substantial and reliable woman than Catherine Earnshaw ever was, and replaced a fantasy affair with a capricious Yorkshire spitfire with a bountiful and prolific one—a real dark haired, dark eyed American temptress … All of my real life forays on the moors have been with her, so our kinship with Yorkshire and Yorkshiremen has been joint, rich, and real.

CATHERINE EARNSHAW, MERLE OBERON, Laurence Olivier, and Wilf Wise are all gone. But not forgotten by an aging romantic.…

11/12/04

Chapter 61

WHERE DOES A LAWYER SHINE BRIGHTEST?

IN 60 YEARS I'VE discovered that a lawyer's talents are tested in several distinct arenas, especially in the courtroom and in the corporate suite. I've been in both and, ironically, felt in each case that my successes represented the ultimate test of a real lawyer's skills.

My first 20 years were spent primarily in the corporate suite and involved not only guiding a growing company through the usual corporate drill, including listing on the NYSE and business overseas, but purchasing or merging with dozens of other companies, including in Greece, The Netherlands, and Puerto Rico.

Even more than in the courtroom, I decided, the true test of a sharp lawyer lies in his skills as a wordsmith and an analyst, with verbal skills honed to their ultimate in drafting contracts like acquisition agreements or recitals in proxy statements. The only way to head off conflict is to foresee it, almost always much more sharply than the clients do. A good lawyer looks for trouble—but before it starts. He heads it off by anticipating the repercussions,, ramifications, and complications that *might* arise, then dealing with them in a balanced fashion and clear language in the contract or securities statement.

I'm reminded of this every time I flip through the pages and pages of "Risk Factors" in a securities filing; lawyers warn that everything bad *could* happen—like Chicken Little—so that no investor can complain that he wasn't warned if the sky does actually fall....

I was very proud of my personal style of acquisition contract, developed with RVW prose and not in old English or from more traditional forms. The ultimate compliments came from opposing parties, a lack of any litigation involving our acquisitions, and occasional copying of my style by other attorneys. I really felt, during my heyday as a one-man Legal Dept., that my contractual and letter-writing skills represented the ultimate mark of a first class attorney.

That is, until I returned to handling medical malpractice trials for two defense firms, then my own. My last 28 years of practice were in the litigation arena—depositions, settlement conferences, hearings, and trials. The literary skills involved writing reports to malpractice insurance claims managers, often long and always detailed narratives and opinions. For hours I dictated them on tape, in the office, in the car, wherever. I saw my role as not only formulating the defense of the case, but also portraying the plaintiff's position—often,

I suspected, better than the plaintiff attorney could do it himself....

The object of the depositions and record reviews and conferences with our experts was obviously to give our clients the most realistic scenario of the case possible, both for settlement evaluation and for setting a proper "reserve" for any possible loss.

But, proud as I was of my analysis and reporting, the ultimate ego trip lay in the conduct of the trial itself—good examination of our client and experts but especially effective cross-examination of the plaintiff and the plaintiff experts, then a lucid summation of the whole case in a favorable light. In 25 years I lost a couple of cases I felt I should have won. But I won a much larger number that I could—or should—have lost. And those were the times when I decided that *this*—the trial arena—is where a lawyer is truly tested, not in the corporate suite or on the dictating machine.

Now, 10 years later, I suspect that good lawyers are tested in all sorts of arenas, anywhere that places a premium on articulation, analysis, anticipation, and assertion....

8/20/11

Chapter 62

My Encounter with
Panamanian Fauna

I HAVE LIVED IN ONLY two foreign countries. One was Korea, where I was stationed for almost a year in 1946. But the living there was in Korea Base Command, a converted Japanese army base. The only truly exotic experiences occurred in Seoul, on Bun Chung. But that's another story.

A boy is very impressionable at age 10. I know I was. And since my mother abandoned my father and flew south whenever the snow fell in Vermont, I had a lot of travel experience from age 10 to age 12. Her migrations took us by car to Miami and by ship (Panama Pacific line), to Cuba, Panama, and California.

I briefly visited schools in Miami and California, which were a lot different from New England schools, but I finished 4th, 5th, and 6th grades in Vermont and became a celebrity of sorts when I returned from the balmy climes and was asked to tell the class about my travels. It was my first—and last—course in public speaking.

My MOTHER AND I stayed part of one winter in Cristobal, Canal Zone—let's call it Panama—where my father's brother was an engineer for the government. That experience distills down to four memory bytes. Three of them were genuinely exotic, starting with the view from my classroom window at school. Nowhere else—and I attended a lot of schools in 20 years—have I ever watched iguanas climbing around in the trees outside. And some of the iguanas in Panama are big, not tourist size, like Cancun.

The only other remnant of my Panama class work is the way I write my cursive "R"—different from everyone else—and the fact that we learned the multiplication tables to 12 down cold, something that our kids never did.

Another unforgettable experience for a boy was the sound of the tires running over hundreds of large land crabs that were strolling across the road at night. I loved it, as any red-blooded young boy would, but my mother hated it, to the amusement of Uncle George and Aunt Lillian.

Another Panamanian custom that seemed strange was practiced in restaurants and bars. I'm sure it's ancient history today, 67 years later. When the adults ordered a beer, the waiter would give the young person a "pony," which was a miniature beer in a glass the size of a vintage Kraft cheese glass. It was a prevalent enough custom so that everyone knew what a "pony" was, but I now wonder if that was a custom invented or created by my Uncle George, who was certainly no toper, or even party boy.

The other unforgettable event would occur any evening when we returned home, no doubt after a "pony" and some crab crushing along the highway. When the kitchen light was turned on, there was a rapid flurry of large brown creatures scurrying in all directions. These were not your small, Miami-size German cockroaches. They must have hiked up from the Amazon jungle— and carried luggage....

As soon as the last one had taken cover, I wondered how many would get to my bed, or be in it. I always looked through my sheets, then worried awhile in bed, wondering what the gang was doing. It was ten years later, at the University of Hawaii, that I learned in my Entomology class that cockroaches disdain contact with humans, and after any encounter clean their antennae....

So, in retrospect, my Panamanian legacy is my very special cursive R, my permanent mastery of the multiplication tables to 12, and a special aversion to cockroaches.

Oh yes, and a special fondness for the nice, gentle iguanas.

2/22/05

Chapter 63

An Unthinkable Win, Too Good To Last

ANY TRIAL LAWYER WOULD know you couldn't win the case. I knew it, too, but the plaintiff attorney wanted way too much money to settle it, maybe more than a jury would award. So in June 1973 I was forced to go to trial.

The facts were against my client. He was a young, marijuana smoking Chinese man who made a left turn in front of an oncoming car. The plaintiff was a 19 year old construction worker who was a passenger in the right front seat, with his wife driving. My client clearly made an unsafe left turn and was hit by the oncoming car at high speed.

The plaintiff hit his knees against the dash, causing his left hip to dislocate so severely that the head of the femur damaged the sciatic nerve, a major nerve that serves the left leg. The neurologist who testified for the plaintiff attorney described the long recovery period for the young plaintiff and the probability that he would suffer permanent pain and dire effects on his ambulation.

Plaintiff attorney proved up $32,000 in medical bills and loss of earnings and predicted future medical bills and loss of earnings in the amount of $164,000. That was before consideration for pain and suffering and permanent disability.

Thirty-two years ago, those were pretty big numbers. And the plaintiff came across as a credible witness, whereas my driver was anything but impressive.

But that wasn't all I had against me. I was as worried about the skills and charms of the plaintiff attorney, Peter Berwick, as the facts of the case. He was a senior partner at Shield and Smith, an experienced trial attorney, and as handsome as a young Robert Redford. In fact, he looked like Redford's brother.

Berwick exuded confidence because he knew his case presented only the question of how much it was worth. He expected a six-figure settlement or verdict—and so did I.

So did the judge, a colorful Southerner named William Murray. I liked his personality and could tell that he admired what must have seemed like bravado on my part to even try the case.

I breathed a large sigh of relief when Judge Murray denied Berwick's motion for a directed verdict, which would have settled the liability issue against me as a matter of law and let the jury merely decide on the amount of damages to be paid to the plaintiff. Judge

Murray left it to the jury to decide both liability and damages. The causation issue was moot because the crash obviously caused the plaintiff's hip dislocation and sciatic neuropathy.

Any trial lawyer would ask how I dealt with the liability issue in my voir dire of the jury, which is the interrogation by the trial attorneys of prospective jurors to get a feel for their experience and attitudes. I don't want to give away too many trade secrets, but it is possible during voir dire to slip a little bit of your argument into your questions about a Juror's background and outlook.

For example, I was able to ask each prospective juror if they felt that a left turner is always the party at fault in a collision—which most people do believe, and rightly so. But no one likes to say "always" or "never", so I used that fact in posing the question. That was really a bit of argument, and a question of law, but Peter Berwick and Judge Murray let me get away with it, no doubt feeling that my case was hopeless, anyway.

There were no surprises during the one week trial. I had an orthopedic surgeon do his best to paint a somewhat brighter future for the plaintiff than Peter Berwick and the plaintiff's neurologist did, but the damage was still serious and I still had an unexcused left turn and an uncharming defendant driver on my hands, so I hoped only that the jury would take it easy on damages. We had already offered $150,000 to settle, and would have gone higher, but Peter Berwick wanted a jury verdict because he thought the trial went well.

The case went to the jury on July 3, 1973, the eve of the July 4 holiday. If they didn't reach a verdict by 4:30 p.m., they would have to come back after the weekend. Time worked in my favor. The jury didn't have enough time to work on the damage figures for medical and loss of earnings, as well as permanent disability. They obviously didn't want to come back after the weekend. So they came in with a verdict in late afternoon and, to my amazement, and that of Judge Murray as well, the vote was 10 to 2 for a defense verdict.

The jury was polled and then dismissed by the judge. Peter Berwick was paralyzed with shock, but recovered enough to rush out into the hall and ask the jurors to return … He tried to have the bailiff round them up, but Judge Murray advised him that he had no power to recall them, that Peter Berwick's only remedy was a motion for a new trial. I left in pleasant shock, but knew we'd be back.

When a judge hears a motion, he always has the moving party present the argument for the motion first. I knew I was cooked when all Judge Murray said was, and I quote, "Mr. Wills, why don't you tell me why I shouldn't grant Mr. Berwick's motion?" I tried, but it was obviously hopeless. The motion was granted and a new trial date set, to start all over.

The insurance carrier for Mr. Chu settled the case

without another trial, apparently for the $150,000 we had offered before and during trial. I never saw Peter Berwick again and Judge Murray retired a few years later. I'm sure that none of the three of us will ever forget that verdict and the scene when Peter Berwick scrambled desperately to get the jury back into the courtroom—as though the judge could make them change their votes, or lecture them, or whatever. It was bizarre, but delightful.

Fleming v. Chu wasn't the last case I won but should have lost. There were also a few that I lost but should have won. Fortunately, very few. But what that case proved is what every experienced trial lawyer knows: a courtroom is just another form of gambling casino where nothing is ever dead certain. All you can do is hope that the ball bounces your way, as it certainly did in July 1973.

2/23/05

Chapter 64

COURTS AND POOLS TO THE FORE

I T WOULD BE HARD TO overestimate the effect on our family of an event in June 1959. That was the month when the Red Hill Tennis Club opened its doors—and courts and pools—to its members. It just so happens that the new club was located in an undeveloped glen just four tenths of a mile from our house, and that our weekend sport had become tennis, unless we were on vacation, in which case it was tennis and snorkeling. The five kids were all under nine years old and had not yet started any organized sports. Tracy was only three months old and Kirk was born over a year later.

We were members of the club for over 40 years and the effects of our family's activities at the club were long term, if not permanent. The club started out with just two tennis courts but three pools, one a wading pool. But it aspired to be a hub of social activity as well as tennis. The bar and the dining room were fully staffed, and in the early days we even had a band for dancing. The founding board envisioned the club as a country club of the old style, with parties, dances, fine dining, and social activities inside—and organized tennis activities outside.

Weekend tennis round robins soon developed and we now have a cupboard full of mugs reflecting our successes. For a short while I served on the Club Board and put out a newsletter and some legal-type letters to members who had problems. And we spent many an enjoyable Monday night up at the Club for a dance instruction program run by an Irishman named Weldon O'Toole. (We may have forgotten everything else, but we can still do the cha cha.)

It wasn't long before the Red Hill Tennis Club had a swim team, organized by the swimming coach and buttressed by a bevy of wildly competitive mothers (and probably a few fathers). The club team began to compete against swim teams of other clubs and swim schools. The Sixties and Seventies spawned lots of private clubs and swim schools that apparently didn't survive. Our boys, and ultimately also Tracy, turned out to be excellent swimmers, so the swim meets added real spice—and some blue ribbons—to our weekends.

Those club swim meets were the forerunners of serious swimming competition for Chris and Kenny at Foothill High School—which, in the Seventies, had the best high school swim team in the U.S. And later, because of tennis lessons, the Red Hill Tennis Club was the source of equally serious high school tennis competition for Tracy and Kirk.

At one point, Kenny was ranked among the top ten butterfliers in the world. Ultimately, he received offers of swim scholarships from both Stanford and UCLA, but chose UCLA ... and Tracy earned a full tennis ride at Cal Poly Pomona, and later taught both high school and college tennis.

Meanwhile, the adults in the family were semi-serious weekend warriors—and sometimes winners—on the tennis courts.

This should be the end of the story—but it isn't. Maralys and I played tennis right into our seventies. More interesting yet, Tracy has now become an age-group tennis competitor who is currently ranked #1, nationally, in 50-and-over doubles.

As for Kenny, whose competitive efforts stopped years ago, the club influence persists. During a weekend competition in Norfolk, Virginia, a number of adults (and 44-year-old Kenny), were invited to participate in an informal swim meet—which included some of the area's top young college swimmers.

At the last minute, urged on by his wife, Kenny decided to compete—to anchor the relay. With only a pair of loose, baggy swim trunks, Kenny was forced to find something to hold up his pants. There he was, poised at the end of the pool, ready to dive in against his competitors—a group of slick young athletes in Speedos.

UCLA to the fore!! Kenny won the race. Later, he was confronted by one of the young males, who asked in surprise, "Aren't you the guy with the trunks held together with rope?"

When a spirited athletic club comes to your neighborhood, you never quite know where the story will end.

2/7/05
8/21/11

Chapter 65

Lament for a Country

IT IS NOT TOO early to grieve. My United States, the country I've respected—make that cherished—for 75 years is about to disappear, as surely as Atlantis sank beneath the sea centuries ago.

Already I can see the waves rolling up and threatening at our shores. The roiling of words like "Clear Skies," spouted and spun to cover the newly-forgiven clouds of mercury spewed from our energy plants and into the atmosphere and oceans. The warming of our seas, egged on by a nation which refuses to cap its clouds of carbon dioxide. The disappearance of magnificent old forests, inevitably succumbing to another jingoistic term, the "Healthy Forests" Initiative.

I hear the lament of our blacks in Florida, disenfranchised by a relentless succession of unspeakable tricks. The cries of the elderly, slowly awakening to the fact that there is no compassion in our government, that the good health of the drug industry supersedes that of its older citizens.

I SEE THE POOR GETTING poorer and more numerous, the newly minted million soon joined by yet another million. I see the elderly forced into HMOs, where all too often only those strong enough to fight for good care actually get it. I see our young men drafted and sent to die in one country after another, for surely Iraq was only the first on our country's list of nations we are "morally bound" to conquer.

Lost in the seas rolling toward our shores will be the right of women to decide the fate of their own bodies ... and the once-decent paychecks of workers in our government-protected businesses, where CEOs flourish and earn 800 times the salaries of their employees. I see the word "compassion" bandied about everywhere, but put into practice nowhere. Even the health and death benefits of our frontline soldiers have recently been offered for cutting.

What is it with our people, anyway? Why do only half of us see what is so obscure to the other half? ... that we are hell bent on returning the leadership of America to a group of egotists who have so far made every mistake it's possible to make. Why do only half of us know that America has begun to sink and will soon go the way of Atlantis?

2004

Chapter 66

HOW THE BOYS BECAME EAGLES

CHRIS ALWAYS WANTED TO fly. Bobby always had to innovate and design. So it was probably no coincidence at all that they became pioneers, activists, and primary developers in the sport of hang gliding.

In the late Sixties, while Bobby was still making double decker bicycles and motorized trash carts, Chris was making a wood-and-paper biplane called The Red Baron, cooking part of the wing framework on our kitchen stove. Accompanied by a clutch of pals and curious fans, he got airborne briefly one weekend by towing on a street in a deserted industrial area. But without a rudder, proper balance, or an engine, the Red Baron had a short life and expired in a bonfire in our back yard.*

Meanwhile, Bobby was turning heads with a 10 foot high "sky bike", with one rider above the other, and a tri-bike, which did the tandem bike one better. If nothing else, Bobby was an innovator and a damned good welder.

ON EARTH DAY IN 1970, Bobby got his picture in the newspaper by riding his sky bike near an amphitheater where Dr. Libby, a Nobel Prize winner, was giving an outdoor lecture. The performance was so distracting that he was asked by security to take his stunt elsewhere.

A National Geographic article in 1971 led to a whole new era of innovation, fabrication, and flight for both Bobby and Chris and their friend, Chris Price. The three of them read about a primitive hang gliding meet in Newport Beach, in an area previously used for a Boy Scout Jamboree, and which later became Fashion Island shopping mall. The gliders were various types of kites and wings obviously home built and producing, at best, very short glides.

In late 1971, or early 1972, the boys obtained some bamboo poles, plastic sheeting, and duct tape and began work in our back yard. The result was a giant triangular bamboo and plastic kite from which the pilot would be suspended by his forearms on a box-like cockpit underneath. By sheer strength the pilot controlled the attitude of the kite by shifting his weight forward or backward on the box frame. The kite was launched by running down a hill into the wind with the nose tilted slightly upward, but not too much, or the kite would stall immediately and drop back down.

The initial flights were from a hill off La Paz Road in Mission Viejo. The glides were short and the trek back up the hill strenuous. The next stage involved a hill overlooking I-5 in San Clemente, above Camino De Estrella, and the kites were now towed back up the hill by Bobby's motorcycle pulling a chariot the boys had built for a race at Foothill High School. Their glides got longer and the spectators and fans more numerous. Photographers started showing up.

It wasn't long before Bill Bennett, "The Australian Birdman," learned of the boys' feats and supplied Bobby with delta wing gliders made with aluminum tubing and Dacron sailcloth. The new kites were controlled by a pilot sitting on a swing seat suspended by ropes, pushing a fixed triangular "control bar" forward or backward to shift the pilot's weight and change the pitch of the kite. A dive required merely a pull toward the pilot, and landing was a controlled stall, with the bar pushed forward. Turns were accomplished by pushing the control bar to one side or the other.

With Bill Bennett's aluminum and Dacron delta wing kites, Bobby became an accomplished hang glider pilot and drew crowds soaring in ridge lift at Palmdale, Torrey Pines, and eventually Hanauma Bay on Oahu. He learned to stay aloft longer and longer by soaring laterally along ridge lift.

In mid-1972, Bobby's first endurance record was a flight of an hour plus at Palmdale, and he became a legendary stunt flyer at Coyote Hills in Northern California, then at Hanauma Bay that summer. He taught pilots how to make turns without diving and soon introduced tandem flying, with two adjoining seats. At Torrey Pines, for the small fee of $5.00, he took courageous strangers up for a thrill of their lifetime, launching off the 300-foot cliff and soaring above the beach below. We can't imagine how many spectators were that intrepid.

His skills produced notoriety but no income from a penurious Bill Bennett, so in early 1973 I formed a corporation called Sport Kites, Inc., so the boys could make and sell their own kites with improved design and flight characteristics. Chris was in college at UCLA, but took enough time off to help set up the company shop and to become an expert pilot himself.

After Chris and Betty Jo were married in August 1973, the whole family went to Maui, then Oahu, where the boys set dramatic new hang gliding records on both islands. After doing terrain and wind pattern studies beforehand, they flew from the top of Haleakala to the sea, a record altitude drop of over 10,000 feet. Then they opened up the ridge in the Koolau range above Makapuu and Waimanalo, where the trade winds went straight up above the 1,200-foot ridge.

Buoyed by their Haleakala triumph, on 9/1/73 Bobby and Chris decided to set a joint endurance record off the cliffs above Makapuu. But after they'd been up a few hours, they got so cold that Chris gave up and landed. Not so Bobby. Instead, Bobby indicated that Chris should find him a jacket. With no idea how we'd get it to him, Chris and I went down to Hawaii Kai and borrowed one from a stranger.

Working feverishly, Chris rolled the jacket into a ball, tied it to a long string, then took off again with his kite. He trailed the bundle behind him in the air and with expert flying by both boys, Bobby flew under Chris, grabbed the string and managed to break it, then with difficulty reined in the jacket.

Bobby's new record was 5 hours and 6 minutes. *

The record and the feat got lots of media coverage and we all feasted on the TV coverage. Yet Bobby wasn't through with Waimanalo.

He did himself one better several days later, establishing an endurance record of 8 hours and 24 minutes that was to last a long time.

By the fall of 1973, hang gliding was getting a lot of press, and the first national competition was held in October at Sylmar, on the East side of the San Fernando Valley. It was covered by ABC and *Sports Illustrated,* among other media, and was later featured in SI.

Using a large sport coach loaned to me by a client we established the Sport Kites headquarters and relished the excitement—watching the kites descend from the mountain top to the landing area target.

Flights were rated for duration, style, and landing skill. Most pilots expected Bobby to win, but he was edged out by his own brother—Chris—in the first championship … Still, Bobby got his revenge a year later at "Escape Country" in Trabuco Canyon, Orange County, a combination hang gliding and motorcycle park. In that second U.S. Championship meet, Bobby finished first and Chris second.

In early 1974, our participation in the sport nearly came to a momentary halt when Eric, not a champion, was killed trying an airborne maneuver he couldn't handle.

Only after a lot of soul-searching did the family decide, as a group, that for Bobby's sake we needed to stick with the sport that had become his whole life.

THE HANG GLIDING ADVENTURES continued in 1975, when the boys and their hang gliding friends won a role in a 20th Century Fox movie by beating out a group of Hollywood stunt men who thought they could hang glide as one more skillful stunt.

The movie, *Skyriders*, was made in Greece and starred Robert Culp, Susannah York, and James Coburn. It involved some dangerous flying from a rock pinnacle down to a monastery precariously perched on a mountain outcropping where a family was held hostage by terrorists. The Wills team did all the flying but were Unit Two, so never faced the camera. Bobby's new wife, Suzette, was also with the gang in Greece and appeared briefly in a circus scene hanging upside down from Bobby's kite.…

We met the boys in England after the movie shoot, where they participated in the British Hang Gliding Championship meet at Mere in Wiltshire, sponsored by BP. A challenging meet, especially for Bobby, who was told he could win only by landing with both feet inside a small chalk bulls eye. He glanced down at his size 14-shoes and said, "Both my feet won't fit inside that circle." When nobody offered a solution, Bobby solved the problem his own way. He won the meet by landing perfectly—on one foot.

AFTER THAT, IN 1975, Bobby was simultaneously the U.S., British, and Canadian hang gliding champion. He continued to design new gliders with better glide ratios and flight characteristics. The Swallowtail was replaced by the Super Swallowtail (SST), then later The Raven. He did some beautiful hang gliding in the IMAX film *To Fly*, filmed by Greg MacGillivray from helicopters along the Na Pali Coast of Kauai.

To the family's horror, in 1977, Bobby himself was killed, blown down by a filming helicopter while making a commercial for Willys Jeep.

CHRIS WENT OFF TO NYU Medical School and later, in his spare time, became a small plane power pilot. He flew ultralight powered gliders, then, ultimately, his own Glastar home-built monoplane. He keeps the plane at Corona airport, and has flown it twice at the

Oshkosh Air Show, once in a demonstration fly-by....

Sport Kites, now called Wills Wing, continues to ship high performance gliders all over the world, but we almost never see a hang glider any more. They fly high, they fly long, and they fly far, but not in highly developed areas like ours. Because of superb skill and equipment, deaths are now few.

Hang gliding cost the lives of both Eric and Bobby, so it would be easy for us to hate the sport and all we saw of it. But we don't.

Those kites were as beautiful up there as giant butterflies, and Bobby and Chris soared like eagles. We don't blame hang gliders for their deaths any more than we blame cars for 45,000 fatal accidents each year.

We do blame a certain helicopter pilot for Bobby's death, but blame doesn't do much good.

The boys simply died while engaged in a beautiful but risky sport.

3/19/05

*This feat, and others, is covered in M's book, *Higher than Eagles*

Chapter 67

GET THE U.S. OUT OF THE U.N?

W HO BUT A REDNECK, a jingoist, a mossback, or an
isolationist would even ask the question?
The world is smaller than ever. Two oceans no longer
serve as moats for us. We are inextricably, inescapably,
ineluctably connected to the rest of the world. Potential
Armageddon is less than an hour away ... And our
economy is irreversibly global.

The only conceivable reasons for abandoning
the UN would be either financial—our contribution
to the UN treasury is a drop in the bucket of the U.S.
budget—or a perverted sense of patriotism and self-determination. In the midst of a frantic election campaign
we are being deluged with that form of dialectic, which
I find repulsive.

In fact, I share Samuel Johnson's iconoclastic view
of patriotism as the last refuge of scoundrels. In our
shrunken world patriotism boils down to a militant
form of colloquialism or provincialism, sadly out of
date and the matrix of war, which we can no longer

afford.

Further, American patriotism is tribute to an amorphous demographic and political morass that defies definition. "America" means far different precepts to diverse segments of the U.S. population. The U.S. is more than polarized—it is fractionated into radically different camps with radically divergent values and goals. I no longer could identify which "America" I would be willing to fight and die for—even if I were so inclined....

Nor is world federalism an answer to the dilemma. It offers allegiance to an even more diverse, polymorphous, fuzzy set of standards and tenets.

I'm afraid the only ism worth our allegiance is the golden rule and Hamlet's soliloquy ... Neither would lead us to xenophobia or war, and neither would require us to die for a cause contrived by politicians.

But in the meanwhile we should not only support the U.N.—we should promote it and celebrate it as our one last hope.

8/2/04

Chapter 69

IF YOU WERE EMPEROR
OF THE UNIVERSE:
What changes would you make?

1. I WOULD DECREE that either the legislature
   or the Supreme Court shall enforce strict
   separation of church and state. Religion is
   infiltrating government under the current
   born-again reformed drunk and party boy and
   his Congressional cronies. There would be no
   Federal or State money to any religious movement, no matter how philanthropic its activities,
   and no theologic recognition in governmental
   proceedings or even on money or monuments
   or buildings.

2. THERE SHALL BE a Federal and State priority
   and emphasis given to family planning, sex
   education, and birth control—the exact
   opposite of what we see now as a result of
   fundamentalist doctrine. Regardless of what
   you hear about moderating birth rates in Japan

and the civilized world, in the next two or three generations the population bomb in Asia, Africa, and Latin America will doom the planet. Potable water will go first, then food, then air, then weather (from global warming).Ironically, lacking urgent governmental action, the only hope for population control will be pestilence, plague, disease, and nuclear holocaust.

3. TRAFFIC SHALL BE controlled exclusively by electronic sensors and computers, not archaic timers. To sit at a red light with no cross traffic is archaic and asinine. In cases of extreme congestion, alternate routes can even be recommended (or mandated). And monorails will be strung on poles erected along the center dividers of the major arterials.

4/23/04

Chapter 70

THE FUTURE OF MEDICINE
WILL SURELY INVOLVE ...

1. A WIDE INCREASE in what is dubbed Minimally-
   Invasive Surgery (MIS), which involves surgery
   through incisions that are much smaller than
   traditional. It is already being promoted for
   total joint replacement, with new instruments
   made by Zimmer and others, and the incisions
   for abdominal surgeries not already possible
   through laparoscopy will become smaller and
   smaller. This reduces recovery time, scarring,
   and, to some extent, the risk of infection.

2. AN EXTENSION OF laser surgery from cosmetic
   procedures to internal organs. A new laser
   vaporization procedure is already threatening
   to become the new gold standard in benign
   prostatic hypertrophy surgery. It dramatically
   reduces recovery time from days to hours. (I
   have had it myself).

3. Other pathology inside the body is already

being treated by laser rather than scalpel or electrocautery.

4. SCANNERS THAT ARE far more intricate and diagnostic, rendering present radiologic, fluoroscopic, and sonographic procedures obsolete. We have just scratched the surface in electronic scanning.

5. ALL PRESCRIPTIONS WRITTEN by doctors transmitted electronically directly to the pharmacy, rather than given in writing to the patient. Plans and equipment are already in the works.

6. AEROSOL TECHNOLOGY FOR the administration of medication directly through the lungs by nebulizer. At least four publicly-owned companies are working on it. (I own stock in all four). This will solve the needle phobia problems and produce instant efficacy.

7. MANY NEW PHARMACEUTICALS developed to control, if not cure, more and more disease and to extend our life expectancy. There are literally hundreds of new drugs in the pipeline, in various stages of development and testing. One or two in a hundred may become "miracle" drugs.

5/15/04

Chapter 71

THE CIVIL LITIGATION PLAGUE:
Letter to *Newsweek*

NEWSWEEK
LETTERS TO THE EDITOR

YOUR PIECE ON THE civil litigation plague ("Civil Wars") is belated but welcome. Your featured activist, Philip Howard, speaks from a more visible pulpit than I did 20 years ago after 35 years of tort and corporate litigation.

I contended then, and still do, that the litigation lottery will continue to grow, and alter American lifestyles, until the scales are balanced with risk for losers on both sides, as is the practice overseas. As long as plaintiffs have no risk at all, and get a free lottery ticket with plaintiff attorneys advancing costs, how can you ever discourage frivolous and blackmail suits? The risks for defendants are both economic and psychological, and very real, even when there is insurance. When plaintiffs lose, they toss their free lottery ticket and walk away, rarely paying a penny of the token costs awarded to successful defendants.

The solution seems as obvious today as it did 20 years ago. Plaintiffs should post litigation bonds to indemnify exonerated defendants for their demonstrable economic losses. And cases requiring expert testimony (e.g. medical, engineering, scientific), should be presented to panels of qualified, independent specialists, not lay juries screened and sanitized by trial lawyers to fit their strategies.

I would remind your readers that lay jury trials are not a constitutional right in civil cases (witness workers' compensation cases), and vary widely in procedure in the 50 small nations we call states. I enjoyed an enviable record in jury trials, but in retrospect believe that the juries reached the wrong decision almost as often as they were right....

12/10/03

Chapter 72

Why Are We Here?
In a Stadium on the 4th of July

If we asked each person here why they came to this huge gathering, I suspect we would get quite a few different answers. The youngest would no doubt say that they are here to see the fireworks. I am, too. Some would say that they came to hear the very jiggy band that we have for you, and maybe even to do a little dancing. Some would admit they like to see a big crowd in action and to watch for oddball outfits or personalities.

Some across the way came to have a picnic with some free entertainment. I doubt that many of this huge crowd came to hear a political speech.

But let me remind you that there is a very large background reason why you are here. You are here because it is our 227th birthday, and when I say "our" I mean the people who are lucky enough to live in the United States of America. How would you like to be living in Afghanistan or Iraq or Liberia or Ethiopia or India? What a different life you would be leading. We are the wealthiest and still the freest country on earth, and hundreds of millions of people in foreign lands would give everything they own to be here.

You hear a lot about the illegal immigration problem in the United States. But you don't hear about that being a big problem in other countries, do you? Ask yourself why, and you'll know why you were fortunate to be born or naturalized as a U.S. citizen.

You are here partly to wish the United States a happy birthday. And, I hope, to recognize how lucky you already are just to be here in Orange County and in this amazing melting pot we call *The United States of America*.

7/4/03

Chapter 73

THE FATAL FALLACY OF CONSERVATISM

A RECENT BOOK BY a Washington right-wing activist was entitled, *Blinded by the Right: The Conscience of an Ex-Conservative.* The surprising revelation to me was that the author, David Brock, is, or was, a closet gay, a member of a group they call the "Laissez-Fairies," who projected their own inner demons onto "the lefties," "the takers," "the coercive utopians," starting with Anita Hill and leading to Bill Clinton. He describes the millions of dollars spent trying to smear Bill Clinton with a love child or mistresses, all of which Linda Tripp and Monica Lewinsky made unnecessary.

But what Brock never articulated is what I believe is the basic, underlying fallacy of conservative belief, namely, that the individual citizen is far more trustworthy and productive than organized government—and that all political and governmental structure is to be opposed, if necessary by force or subversion. While I am no fan of governmental efficiency or integrity, I submit that the age-old Emersonian concepts of individual self government and individual self realization are one hundred years out of date, along with our other Frontier notions of unlimited resources and unimpeachable environment.

The concepts that governed small New England towns and settled the West one hundred fifty years ago, built on The Bible and the rifle and a pioneering spirit, are no longer operative in the year 2002.

You don't have to be cynical to reach that conclusion. You only have to observe the news. The Watts and Detroit riots, the Enron and Global Crossings scandals, the Montana "Freemen," Ruby Ridge rebels, Timothy McVeigh, the Unabomber, the anthrax mailer, and the hundreds of thousands of violent criminals in prison are all examples of individual freedom gone rotten. Yet all would ridicule governmental controls and political institutions.

No one today would conceive of unregulated vehicular traffic, the norm in the 19th century. No stop signs, no traffic signals, no 2-inch-thick vehicle code.

Would you risk a community without an armed police force or an organized fire department, or even zoning and land use laws? Or without Federal regulation of aircraft, ships, and immigration … lax and sloppy though it may be?

Why then do conservatives still favor scrapping gun control laws, utility and airline rate regulation, and workplace safety laws? Are they really willing to let corporate executives and individual entrepreneurs and farmers make their own rules of competition and employment practices? And are they willing to live in a community where residents observe no rules regarding land use, firearm use, and vehicle use?

I doubt it. But the conservative remains basically opposed to group controls, whether local, national, or international, and is basically willing to trust to individual ethics and personal responsibility.

It's a lovely but antiquated philosophy in a world headed for 10 billion population, a degraded environment, threats of famine and plague, and a growing distrust of the United States. The more populous our cities, the greater the frictions between neighbors. The shrinking of the world through global telecommunication can only incite the "have-nots" of the Third World further against the "haves" of the world we know. And the resurgence of religious fervor here or abroad can only inflame passions further and increase the risk of wars and the need for ever more population controls.

No, in this century, the conservatives are dead wrong and ultimately dangerous. I was one for over 50 years, but based my views on family legacy and visions of a Vermont village governed by a town council and town meetings.

The world is a far more fractionated and dangerous place than it was even 50 years ago. And, unfortunately for our children and grandchildren, we now have an administration devoted to a libertarian, America-First, Christian fundamentalist philosophy that is as dangerous as it is regressive. Fifty years ago it would have been labeled "reactionary," rock-ribbed, blue-nosed, and isolationist. Today it is just plain regressive and dangerous.

4/12/02

Chapter 74

A Plea for Common Sense

ALL AROUND ME, I see idiocy taken seriously. I observe intelligent people listening attentively to the reasonings of "screw-loosers." What court, for instance, could possibly entertain the notion that companies in the 21st century ought to pay reparations to blacks whose ancestors were damaged a hundred years ago? … and why should today's people of color imagine they've got anything coming to them from a society that now bends over backwards not to discriminate?

Why does the American Bar Association—or the government—sanction Class Action Suits which benefit nobody except the lawyers?

Who is the idiot who dreamed up zero tolerance … or worse, who are the Principals who follow it to the absurd letter—like the principal who suspended the second-grader who brought to school a knife to cut his birthday cake … or the one who transferred to a different high school the trombonist who used a screw-driver to adjust his instrument? Can't these people *think*? Doesn't a child's intent mean anything? As practiced, zero tolerance too often means zero common sense.

Who can possibly stand up for Three Strikes when in practice it hasn't meant what the voters thought it meant—that felons who threaten bodily harm to others ought to be put away for a long time. Instead, when applied to the letter of California law, a third strike can—and has—meant that an offender who steals a few tapes from Kmart can be given 25-five years to life … a penalty which, incidentally, costs taxpayers upwards of $25,000 a year. Is this common sense?

How can a leader like Israel's Ariel Sharon be so stupid as to imagine if he crushes and kills enough of his enemies the rest will lie down and be nice people? For that matter, why does any parent believe the more he beats his kid the better adult he'll be? I still remember the comments of a relative who told us with some pride that her parents had beaten her regularly, and look at me, it's never hurt me … when in fact she's one of the witchiest women I know, and to my knowledge has no friends in the community in which she's lived for 40 years.

Why does our government knock itself out and placate its enemies trying to procure oil, when common sense says we could spend reasonable amounts of money to reduce our oil needs to the supply within our borders. Solar panels on the roof of every house, plus 50-miles-per-gallon cars would do it. And both are technologically feasible.

2/14/02

Chapter 75

CARPE DIEM

CARPE DIEM, MY FRIENDS, CARPE DIEM like you never have before.

I'm not a senior who suffers from the latest disorder-of-the-month, senior depression syndrome. But I spend a lot of time reading the mainstream media and have never recovered from a Stanford course in physical and economic geography and another in advanced statistics at UCLA. And I can't ignore the following statistics, try as I may.

1. No empire in recorded history has lasted over 400 years.

2. The American Empire, if an empire it be, is now approximately 225 years old.

3. At no prior time in history have non-dominant nations had weapons of mass destruction, to use W's favorite phrase, or individuals had the capacity to kill thousands, or even millions, of humans and throw a nation into turmoil.

4. The technology we developed to win World War II is now available to rogue nations and even to sophisticated, dedicated individuals who can afford technical staff.

5. Telecommunication now blankets the globe, so that enemies can monitor each other's activities at will and in real time. Even the ragtag Taliban had computers and TV.

6. As a democracy dedicated to free speech and an informed electorate, we telegraph our every move through the media, attempting only to shield our latest technology from public view through security laws and clearance procedures.

7. The Rosenbergs, Pollocks, and Hansons have made it clear that our security systems are porous and that there will never be a shortage of espionage recruits. Between the tireless efforts of the media and a continuous parade of spies, it's doubtful that there is any such thing as top secret in this country. Even White House security is as leaky as an old boat, though the current commander is attempting to thicken the veil of secrecy.

8. One out of five people on earth is a Muslim, or lives in a Muslim culture. Only one out of 20 is an American. The Muslim numbers are growing faster than the American numbers, even

counting our uncontrolled immigration.

9. The U.S. is both politically and economically aligned with Israel, to the point where the radical Islamic world regards us as partners. Israel is the #1 recipient of U.S. foreign aid, reportedly to the tune of 3 billion dollars annually. On a theory of stabilizing the Mideast against Israeli expulsion, the U.S. has supplied Israel with enough armament to make it the most heavily armed Mideast nation.

10. The U.S. acquires a substantial portion of its oil from the Arab countries including, legally or otherwise, from Iraq. Imports from Israel are negligible.

11. The Palestinians are a pathetic lot, both economically and politically. They don't even have a recognized state. Their boundaries are set by Israel and are being continually revised by Israeli settlements. They control neither their boundaries nor their destiny. Increasingly, they are a desperate and teeming mass of humanity.

12. The Israelis are now seen by much of the world as brutalizing the Palestinians by oppressive military force. Suicide bombers and slingshots are no match for tanks, rockets, helicopters, and bulldozers. The kill ratio is somewhere between 10 and 20 to one. The Arabic world will soon

conclude that Israeli action in Ramallah and Jenin by an invading force amounted to massacre and atrocities bordering on genocide. The Israelis are now regarded as the mortal enemy of the Islamic world. And the U.S., because of our perceived partnership with Israel is reaping some of the hatred and vows for revenge.

13. The prayer uttered by the AWOL 9/11 crew member, Moussaoui, this week—for the destruction of the U.S.—will be shared by thousands of Palestinians and radical Muslims all over the world. George W. won't be able to find and eradicate them any more than he did Osama bin Laden. So the question is going to be, How can we head off more 9/11 attacks— and worse? And if Commander Bush attacks any other Muslim country, Iraq or otherwise, with or without Allied participation, you had better stay tuned for some very nasty days ahead…!

Meanwhile, *carpe diem*! Every day of our present bounty and personal safety is a gift not to be taken lightly.

4/23/02

Chapter 76

LETTER TO CHRISTOPHER COX

Honorable Christopher Cox
U.S. House of Representatives
Washington, D.C.   May 15, 2002

You were a speech writer for Ronald Reagan and a favorite for appointment to the U.S. Court of Appeals. You are a Committee Chairman and one of the fair-haired young stalwarts in the Republican party. So it goes without saying that you are intelligent and have a wide open future.

We are therefore astounded that you vote against all efforts to allow Federal funds to be used for family planning programs domestically and overseas (versions of the so-called Mexico City rule). There is little hope for this planet, and certainly none for our standard of living, if population trends continue in this century. The only hope for moderating population growth certainly lies in education and medicine, not religious doctrine or wishful thinking. To require all Federal money to be channeled to programs preaching abstinence until marriage is about as effective as supporting witchcraft, requiring a loyalty oath, or promoting the Tooth Fairy. It turns a blind eye to both pre-marital sex, celebrated and almost promoted by the media, and unwanted pregnancies *after* marriage—a major component of the population bomb.

The Republican "abstinence till marriage" platform is a good moral precept but about as effective in preventing unfortunate pregnancies as Nancy Reagan's "Just Say No" campaign has been in combating the other teenage scourge—drugs.

After 40 years of voting Republican, we cannot comprehend why the Republican party seems to be blind to the fact that:

1. Family size is a critical factor in determining standard of living for a family;

2. almost all educated and responsible adults limit the size of their families (and prevent premarital pregnancy) by family planning and/or birth control measures;

3. vast segments of the world population, including a few segments of the U.S. population, produce unwanted or excessive pregnancies because of a lack of family counseling and/or birth control means;

4. (right or wrong), television and the movies and

adolescent peer groups all recognize, and almost promote, premarital and extramarital sex, to the point where virginity at marriage is the exception, not the rule;

5. unwanted pregnancies and unchecked population are at the heart of most of our other social and environmental maladies—pollution, global warming, hunger, child abuse, domestic violence, and limited education, not to mention abortion.

As a leading stalwart in the Republican party, and a man with a future in government, we hope you will rethink your position on family planning and family counseling and work toward a society where all new babies are wanted babies, welcome babies, with eager and proud parents.

Sincerely,
Robert V. Wills

Chapter 77

THE "BLOWBACK" WAR

My initial reaction to the dastardly 9/11 attack was the same as almost everyone's—blast Osama bin Laden and Afghanistan back to the Stone Age, and detain anyone who looks or sounds Arab ... We were the first to get the stars and stripes out front at our son's house in Norfolk, where we were trapped for five extra days.

But then we began seeing the portrait of Afghanistan as a bombed-out hulk of a third world country with a wretched population, and Afghani expatriates—and the Russian leaders—warned us that the country would be another, very mountainous Vietnam. Even Bush has backed away from talk of an all-out military assault, and we have finally discovered our natural allies already on the ground in Afghanistan—the Northern Alliance. The NATO members have joined our team, presumably for military operations as well.

So things are looking up for a broad campaign against the Taliban and Al-Qaida. Hopefully we will mobilize and reinforce the Northern Alliance and recruit dozens of disillusioned Taliban members who decide to betray bin Laden. I hope our attack will be two-pronged: logistic and tactical support for the Northern Alliance and a humanitarian/psychological campaign to win the Afghan population away from the Al-Qaida. I do agree that we must get bin Laden, dead or alive, preferably dead, if only because we will look like a paper tiger if we don't.

And while we are wrapping ourselves in the flag and vowing revenge, I am reminded of the following ugly facts that Americans prefer to forget:

1. The killing of thousands of noncombatant men, women, and children in New York was a crime against humanity, but far from the first or the biggest:

    a. In August 1945, the U.S. killed hundreds of thousands of civilians in Hiroshima and Nagasaki, admittedly during wartime, but with a secret new weapon.

    b. Dresden—April 1945—the Allied bombers killed over 200,000 civilians in one night. Dresden was not a serious military target and the purpose of the raid was demoralization of the German public.

    c. The original "day of infamy" was a sneak attack

intended to start a war, but was against military targets and killed only 2,600.

2. It is not quite accurate to say that the Sept. 11, 2001 destruction was the start of an undeclared war. Bin Laden had already attacked two U.S. embassies in Africa, a destroyer in Oman, and the World Trade Center once before (eight years ago). Our intelligence people now admit that they were aware that attacks in the U.S. were being planned for several years. Bin Laden actually declared war on the U.S. years ago.

3. The U.S. is admittedly the most powerful nation on earth, but, by any traditional criteria, has not won any of its last three wars.

   a. Korea was a brutal, expensive war that left Korea split in half and the Communists in control of the north to this day, clearly an undesirable outcome. Kim Il Sung died of old age.

   b. Vietnam was a military and psychological disaster which resulted in our retreat under fire and horrible psychological scars. Ho Chi Minh died of old age....

   c. The Persian Gulf War lasted only a few days, cost billions, and left Saddam Hussein in power and as much a threat today as 10 years ago.

4. Osama Bin Laden and many of his lieutenants

were trained in military tactics by our own
CIA, so that they could defeat the Russian
invasion twenty years ago (which they did). Bin
Laden knows how we think in terms of military
strategy and he knows that our country has lax
security because of our celebrated freedoms.
So he won Round One and has us scrambling
(probably into a major recession.)

So we should not promise a total victory over
Muslim extremism and terrorism, because the last total
victory we had in war was 56 years ago. There are over
one billion one hundred million Muslims in the world,
most of whom resent the fact that we have armed Israel
to the teeth while Palestinians fight with stones and
while Israel continues to annex land. As long as the
Muslim world sees us as Israel's partner and protector,
and as long as Muslims control the bulk of the world's
oil, we will be sitting on a powder keg.

But the rest of the civilized world despises terrorism and treachery as well, so we would have to predict
the downfall of the Taliban in time, probably at great
cost to us.

9/28/01

Chapter 78

THE TOPSY-TURVY SOCIETY

EVERY YEAR *PARADE* MAGAZINE publishes a gallery of people representing a broad range of occupations, with dozens of small portraits listing their names, home towns, and annual incomes. The incomes vary from a low five-figures to a staggering eight figures. You would recognize most of the faces associated with eight-figure incomes, and many of those reporting seven figures.

Without requiring a word of prose, the gallery represents the most scathing and graphic portrayal possible of a society which has its values in total disarray. How could anyone explain to a Founding Father why the nation they conceived values a 7-foot basketball player or a rock musician or a movie star as having 400 times the worth of a university professor or a concert musician or a primary school teacher—and 150 times the worth of a surgeon or an oncologist. Semi-articulate athletes and drug-fuzzy rock stars and giddy actresses are household names, while educators and scientists and researchers labor in quiet obscurity at five-figure salaries.

There must be an explanation for the radical disparity in income between so-called superstars who perform in arenas and stadiums and movie theaters—and those who labor quietly in factories, hospitals, schools, offices, and concert halls. But it's an explanation that doesn't bode well for the future of this 225-year-old republic. It's a salute to flash and dash and clash—and celebrity ... a tribute to people who get into Halls of Fame and are given sidewalk stars, not Nobel Peace Prizes and Pulitzer Prizes.

I don't believe it can be explained as an economic accident or an anomaly. No—in a Capitalist society money goes where people aim it. Millions more idolize a seven-foot basketball player—who consequently earns $20 million per year—than a teacher or a policeman who earns $50,000 per year. Salaries reflect what people are willing to pay for the product, so team owners, rock fans, school boards, and corporate executives pay their performers accordingly.

7/23/01

Chapter 79

WHAT AM I?

IN A SOCIETY ADDICTED to labels I don't know what to call myself, politically and economically. I'm registered Republican, but everything the Republican party now preaches makes my hair stand on end. I'm confident that we have the dumbest president since Coolidge and that Trent Lott is a mossback reactionary. But Nader gives me a rash and populists give me the creeps.

Libertarians are a century out of touch with reality. Labor unions are in constant need of economic education. The man on the street is inexcusably and blissfully ignorant. And the traditional Democrats want more government programs—which get bloated and sloppy.

I guess I'll just call myself an Independent—and run the risk of being labeled indecisive and ineffectual, if not cowardly.

7/18/01

Chapter 80

On Faith-Based Flim-flam: Fountain of Beneficence or Constitutional Tar Pit?

Unfortunately, the separation of church and state is not as clearly mandated in the First Amendment as it should be. The members of the first Congress in 1791 merely prohibited Congress from making any laws "respecting an establishment of religion or prohibiting the free exercise thereof."

A country formed after the centuries of tyranny by the Catholic Church on the Continent and the Church of England in The British Empire should have mandated clearly that religion in any form should have no role in our government and shall receive no form of monetary support from that government. If the Founding Fathers had not been so terse in setting out the rules, we wouldn't have a right wing executive now threatening to funnel Federal money into so-called faith-based charitable programs, as one way of rewarding the fundamentalist right wing that worked hard to elect him.

The last thing this government needs is a body infiltrated with right wing Christians who claim they are guided by some higher source known only to them —and who therefore claim a clearer vision of our welfare and destiny than we pagans enjoy.

May heaven—or the Supreme Court—protect us from our born-again leader and all others who have seen a light we can't all see and who want to govern our lives accordingly.

7/17/01

Chapter 81

LEERING LEGIONS OF LOOKY-LOOS

I'VE ALWAYS LOVED THAT anonymous witticism, "Of all sexual perversions, abstinence is the strangest." Thanks to the Puritanical, then the Victorian, attitudes in this country, it would appear that the U.S. is the most frustrated, and therefore the most sex-obsessed, nation in the world.

Americans write about sex, make movies about sex, and talk about sex ad nauseam. They take pills and use devices. They visit flourishing pornographic web sites. They fantasize about sex.

Isn't it too bad they don't just do it more and shut up about it?

5/29/00

Chapter 82

THE OTHER CRITICAL COVERAGE:
Memo to the Wills Clan

H ERE'S A HORROR STORY that should teach all
of you a lesson and make you check your auto
insurance policies. It has to do with uninsured drivers,
of which there are now tens of thousands in California
because of the recession and a high unemployment rate.

The most important coverage in your auto policy
is the liability coverage, which should be a minimum of
$100,000. (I buy 250,00/500,000). If you are at fault, you
don't want to get sued and not have enough coverage.

But the second most important coverage in your
policy is the coverage for uninsured driver loss. This
is coverage U or W and most people pay no attention
to it, but instead settle for the State-required minimum of $15,000/$5,000. This is a huge mistake when
an uninsured driver can total your $50,000 car or put
your passenger in the hospital. The uninsured motorist
coverage isn't that expensive, but it is going up now
because of what is happening in California.

Even though proof of liability insurance

(minimum coverage—totally inadequate), is required for vehicle registration, some drivers let policies lapse between registrations, and others—many others—con the DMV with forged or altered insurance certificates. Whiteout and a photocopy do the job. So we are now told that somewhere between 15% and 20% of all California drivers are on the road today without liability insurance—and many of the rest have completely inadequate minimum limits.

The first rule is to have a decent level of uninsured motorist coverage—in my opinion, at least $100,000. But the second rule was learned by a couple who were recently rear-ended on a Freeway off ramp. They saw that the couple in the van that hit them was horrified, so they pulled into the nearest open area, only to see the other van speed away. They gave chase and called 911, but were told not to continue the chase or they might get shot or beat up. So they never got the license plate number for the guilty van.

Long story short. The Auto Club refused to give them coverage for their damage because they could not identify the other vehicle, and thereby establish that it was uninsured. So they ate the $900 repair bill themselves and the guilty party went off scot-free.

The third rule (from an old auto accident defense attorney), is to go nowhere without a camera in the car and never leave an accident scene without taking photos. Even a throwaway flash camera in the glove compartment will do. People lie, or have defective memories. If you have lying opponents or obdurate insurance reps, photos are your best friend. A throw-away camera (usually film type), and a dozen photo prints might save you thousands of dollars. I have fended off a couple of minor claims by taking photos at the scene.

All of this good advice came out of a reading of today's paper—and decades of listening to people shade or alter the truth....

11/29/09

Chapter 83

Squibs

The RVW Propinquity Corollary:
The need for governmental activity is inversely proportional to the moral integrity of the populace—and directly proportionate to the density of the population.

9/28/02

"Patriotism" and War Heroes:
The only form of mortal combat that is rational to a sane human is combat with a known, visible adversay. Killing of unkown, unseen strangers on behalf of a capricious political body—which will probably change sides within a decade—is murder, regardless of the medals and benefits you may receive. (Exhibit A—Germany and Japan.)

5/22/01

We spend the first third of our lives abusing our bodies—and the last third trying to salvage them....

6/23/93

A good lover approaches his lady like a violin

247

virtuoso approaches his Stradivarius—with loving tenderness and gentleness. He then plays a lilting barnyard tune.

9/17/99

ROBERT V. WILLS TRAVELED extensively as a youth because of a Naval Officer father and a travel-prone mother. Multiplicity also characterized his college years, resulting in three degrees after four universities. His final degree was in Law at UCLA. That led to two different legal careers, one as General Counsel and Officer of a Big Board corporation and the second as a medical malpractice trial lawyer with his own law firm in Southern California.

His previous book, *Lawyers are Killing America*, was a plea for genuine tort reform in the U.S. This new volume contains essays on myriad areas of the American social and political landscape, reflecting a unique and unorthodox perspective on the passing parade.

Reader enthusiasm is crucial for any author to succeed. If you enjoyed the book, please consider leaving a review at the online book seller's page for the book. Even if it's only a few lines, it would make all the difference and would be very much appreciated.

If you liked this book please look for the next volume: *Gaining a Little Altitude: Leaving Ideology on the Ground* by Robert V. Wills.

www.ingramcontent.com/pod-product-compliance
Lightning Source LLC
Chambersburg PA
CBHW031831090426
42741CB00005B/202